THE EXPLORER'S GUIDE TO ALGONQUIN PARK

TEXT AND PHOTOGRAPHS BY

MICHAEL RUNTZ

The BOSTON MILLS PRESS

For Harrison and Dylan:
may we have the wisdom to ensure that
Algonquin and other wild places
eternally remain for you and all others to explore.

Revised edition printed in 2000 by
BOSTON MILLS PRESS
132 Main Street
Erin, Ontario N0B 1T0
Tel 519-833-2407
Fax 519-833-2195
e-mail books@bostonmillspress.com
www.bostonmillspress.com

An affiliate of
STODDART PUBLISHING CO. LIMITED
34 Lesmill Road
Toronto, Ontario, Canada
M3B 2T6
Tel 416-445-3333
Fax 416-445-5967
e-mail gdsinc@genpub.com

Distributed in Canada by
GENERAL DISTRIBUTION SERVICES LIMITED
325 Humber College Boulevard
Toronto, Canada M9W 7C3
Orders 1-800-387-0141 Ontario & Quebec
Orders 1-800-387-0172 NW Ontario & other provinces
e-mail cservice@genpub.com

Distributed in the United States by
GENERAL DISTRIBUTION SERVICES INC.
PMB 128, 4500 Witmer Industrial Estates
Niagara Falls, New York 14305-1386
Toll-free 1-800-805-1083
Toll-free fax 1-800-481-6207
e-mail gdsinc@genpub.com
www.genpub.com

04 03 02 01 00   5 6 7 8 9

Canadian Cataloquing in Publication Data

Runtz, Michael W. P.
The explorer's guide to Algonquin Park

rev'd ed.
Includes bibliographical references and index.

ISBN 1-55046-319-5

1. Algonquin Provincial Park (Ont.) – Guidebooks.
2. Natural history – Ontario – Algonquin Provincial Park - Guidebooks.
3. Outdoor life - Ontario - Algonquin Provincial Park - Guidebooks. I. Title.

FC3065.A4R87 2000   917.13'147   C00-930649-8
F1059.A4R87 2000

THE CANADA COUNCIL | LE CONSEIL DES ARTS
FOR THE ARTS | DU CANADA
SINCE 1957 | DEPUIS 1957

We acknowledge for their financial support of our publishing program the
Canada Council, the Ontario Arts Council, and the Government of Canada
through the Book Publishing Industry Development Program (BPIDP).

Design: Brant Cowie and Associates
Maps and Plates: Robert A. Bracken
Front Cover Photograph: The Barron River Canyon

Printed and bound in Canada

Contents

For Harrison and Dylan:
may we have the wisdom to ensure that
Algonquin and other wild places
eternally remain for you and all others to explore.

Revised edition printed in 2000 by
BOSTON MILLS PRESS
132 Main Street
Erin, Ontario N0B 1T0
Tel 519-833-2407
Fax 519-833-2195
e-mail books@bostonmillspress.com
www.bostonmillspress.com

An affiliate of
STODDART PUBLISHING CO. LIMITED
34 Lesmill Road
Toronto, Ontario, Canada
M3B 2T6
Tel 416-445-3333
Fax 416-445-5967
e-mail gdsinc@genpub.com

Distributed in Canada by
GENERAL DISTRIBUTION SERVICES LIMITED
325 Humber College Boulevard
Toronto, Canada M9W 7C3
Orders 1-800-387-0141 Ontario & Quebec
Orders 1-800-387-0172 NW Ontario & other provinces
e-mail cservice@genpub.com

Distributed in the United States by
GENERAL DISTRIBUTION SERVICES INC.
PMB 128, 4500 Witmer Industrial Estates
Niagara Falls, New York 14305-1386
Toll-free 1-800-805-1083
Toll-free fax 1-800-481-6207
e-mail gdsinc@genpub.com
www.genpub.com

04 03 02 01 00   5 6 7 8 9

Canadian Cataloguing in Publication Data

Runtz, Michael W. P.
The explorer's guide to Algonquin Park

rev'd ed.
Includes bibliographical references and index.

ISBN 1-55046-319-5

1. Algonquin Provincial Park (Ont.) – Guidebooks.
2. Natural history – Ontario – Algonquin Provincial Park - Guidebooks.
3. Outdoor life - Ontario - Algonquin Provincial Park - Guidebooks. I. Title.

FC3065.A4R87 2000   917.13'147   C00-930649-8
F1059.A4R87 2000

THE CANADA COUNCIL | LE CONSEIL DES ARTS
FOR THE ARTS | DU CANADA
SINCE 1957 | DEPUIS 1957

We acknowledge for their financial support of our publishing program the
Canada Council, the Ontario Arts Council, and the Government of Canada
through the Book Publishing Industry Development Program (BPIDP).

Design: Brant Cowie and Associates
Maps and Plates: Robert A. Bracken and Deborah Burke
Front Cover Photograph: The Barron River Canyon

Printed and bound in Canada

Acknowledgments

THERE ARE COUNTLESS PEOPLE over the years who have shared their knowledge and passion for Algonquin Park with me. In particular I must thank Ron Tozer and Dan Strickland for not only tutoring me but also for generously putting up with me over the many years I worked at the old Park Museum and, more recently, at the Visitor Centre.

As well, a sincere thanks to Ron Tozer and Nancy Checko for critically reviewing the text and offering many valuable suggestions. Rory MacKay and Jack Mihell were treasure houses for information on Algonquin's history. Other individuals to whom I am indebted include Larry Weller, Larry Cobb, Graham and Lee Forbes, Bill Crins, Henry Checko, Jack Borrowman, Ernie Martelle, Ron Stephenson, Bill and Richard Swift, and Gerhard Schinke.

Special thanks to Bob Bracken, friend and artist extraordinaire, for the excellent artwork and maps that he produced for this book.

And last but never least, my heartfelt gratitude goes to my wife, Heather, and son, Harrison, for understanding and sharing my love for "the Park."

It is hard to believe that seven years have passed since the Explorer's Guide to Algonquin Park first came out. The many positive comments I have received from users suggest to me that the book is fulfilling its purpose. However, in the past seven years many changes have taken place in the Park and a revision is now due.

A very special thanks is owed to Ron Tozer for his invaluable assistance in preparing this revision. Additionally, Deborah Burke provided the map to the Kingscote Lake area and Bob Bracken the plate of Algonquin deciduous tree leaves. Also, thank you to Rhonda Dalrymple for additional and very useful comments.

I FELL IN LOVE with Algonquin Park on my very first visit. That was in 1957 when my family came to see the absurdly bold deer, which, in those days, drew much attention to the Park. I am sure my parents could never have predicted that from this initial magical excursion an irrepressible obsession would grow.

Many special features set Algonquin Park apart: the maze of sparkling waterways that leads into the wilds; the moose, loons, wolves and other untamed creatures that so readily tolerate our intrusions; the crisp night skies where the aurora dances among the blazing stars. It is also a place where we can share our passion for wilderness with kindred souls.

I have worked many years in Algonquin and have explored its wild recesses as a naturalist, canoeist, biologist and photographer, which has given me a certain familiarity with the Park and its visitors. Over the years the comments and questions of other Park users, ranging from novice campers to serious birders, made it clear there was a real need for a book of this nature. While many of the answers to popular questions could be found in the various excellent Park publications, no single reference pooled the existing information. As well, other specific questions could only be answered by finding the right person to ask or else remained unanswered. This book was written with those needs in mind, and I hope it is an aid to your enjoyment of this incomparable Park.

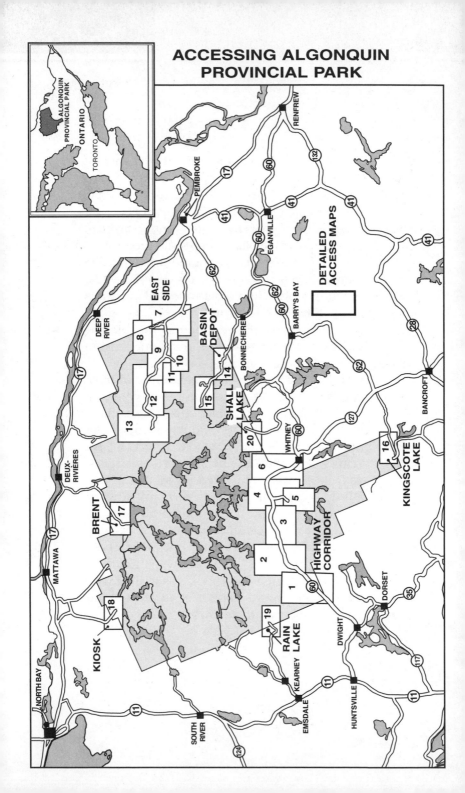

ACCESSING ALGONQUIN
PROVINCIAL PARK

ALGONQUIN PROVINCIAL PARK

ONTARIO

TORONTO

DETAILED ACCESS MAPS

EAST SIDE

BASIN DEPOT

SHALL LAKE

HIGHWAY CORRIDOR

KINGSCOTE LAKE

BRENT

KIOSK

RAIN LAKE

RENFREW

PEMBROKE

EGANVILLE

BARRY'S BAY

BONNECHERE

BANCROFT

WHITNEY

DWIGHT

DORSET

HUNTSVILLE

KEARNEY

EMSDALE

SOUTH RIVER

NORTH BAY

MATTAWA

DEEP RIVER

DEUX-RIVIÈRES

W ELCOME TO ALGONQUIN PROVINCIAL PARK, the oldest and third largest park in Ontario (only Polar
Bear and Wabakimi are larger). For tmore than 100
years this magnificent Park has captured the hearts of
millions of visitors who have canoed its clear waters
and hiked its endless forests. This extraordinary area
was formally set aside in 1893, thanks to the efforts
and incredible foresight of Alexander Kirkwood and
James Dickson. These men, one a government clerk
and the other a land surveyor, recognized this highland
area as the source of a number of major rivers and the
essential habitat for a wide array of wildlife. Water and
wildlife, the special features recognized a hundred
years ago, are the same attributes that currently attract
hundreds of thousands of people annually to the Park.

People are drawn to Algonquin for a number of
reasons, one of which is certainly its immense size.
With 7,700 square kilometres encompassing endless
forests and over a thousand sparkling lakes, the Park
offers limitless outdoor recreational opportunities.

Another reason is the amazing diversity of life
found here — over 265 species of birds, 40 types of
mammals and 1,000 species of plants flourish in the
Park. Even more striking is the mixture of species.
Southern animals such as white-tailed deer and
Scarlet Tanagers occur in proximity to moose and
Spruce Grouse, true "northerners." In many ways
Algonquin is a naturalist's dream come true.

But why such a diverse array of flora and fauna? The
answer lies in the Park's location and in its geological
history. Algonquin is situated in a vegetation transition
zone known as the Great Lakes–St. Lawrence Forest

Western Algonquin boasts hills covered with hardwood forests and waterways fringed with boreal bogs.

Region. Here temperatures and the growing season are adequate to support a mixture of plants, a number more southern in distribution. Furthermore, the Park is located on a dome where elevations (reaching 585 metres above sea level) intensify temperature extremes, allowing for the establishment of boreal plants.

The last Ice Age also had an important impact on the region. When the glaciers finally retreated a mere 11,000 years ago, a layer of rocks, gravel, sand and silt was deposited over the western highlands. This glacial till traps moisture, which allows hardwood forests to grow. Sugar maple, yellow birch, American beech and ironwood thrive on these hillsides. These hardwood forests change to brilliant hues in the autumn, putting on a show of colour rarely equalled elsewhere.

Great beds of sand, deposited by glacial rivers that flowed through much of the Park's East Side, support a much different forest. This soil fails to trap moisture and thus remains relatively dry. The dry conditions, amplified by a slight rain shadow created by the higher elevations of the West Side, favour the growth of trembling aspen and white, red and jack pines.

Coniferous forests also abound in other areas. All through Algonquin cool shorelines are fringed by spruces, balsam fir, white cedar and eastern hemlock. Floating sphagnum bogs, wherever solid enough, support the spindly spires of black spruce and the delicate contours of tamarack.

In turn this incredible mosaic of forests sustains the rich array of animal life for which Algonquin is famous. Today the Park is one of the finest moose-viewing areas in the world and boasts one of the most accessible wolf populations anywhere. This abundance of life affords excellent photographic opportunities. I speak from personal experience — four of my books are fully illustrated with photographs taken in Algonquin and another four in part.

The forests we see nowadays, however, are much different from those encountered by the region's first visitors. Enormous white pines cloaked the eastern side of Algonquin and like giants towered here and there above the hardwoods of the western uplands. It was these monstrous pines with trunks straight as arrows that captured the attention of the early logging industry. As early as the 1830s, axes rang in these forests as the monstrous pines were felled. Thousands of men spent their winters here, cutting the trees, removing the bark and outer wood in a process known as "squaring," and hauling the timbers to frozen lakes. These hardy men lived in the "camboose," a large log cabin that was situated close to the cutting area. Meals were cooked over a central fireplace, and the fifty or so hardy men ate and slept in the camboose for the duration of the long, cold season. In spring the camps broke up and the timbers were "driven" down swollen rivers to the mighty Ottawa.

By the late 1800s the supply of big pines began to vanish, but a need for other trees soon arose. Smaller trees, undoubtedly scorned by earlier loggers, were eagerly harvested as the demand for sawn lumber quickly grew. New logging camps, more modern in construction than the camboose camps over which they were frequently erected, sprang up over the ensuing years. Logs still thundered down rivers in spring but now also left the newly created Park by rail. In addition to logs, the Ottawa, Arnprior and Parry Sound Railway (built between 1894 and 1896 by J. R. Booth, a powerful lumber baron) transported sawn lumber produced in mills located in the Park.

The railway was also important as a means for fishermen and other recreationists to visit Algonquin. As the fame of the Park spread, lodges opened along the rail line and summer residences sprung up on many of the lakes. The highway arrived in the mid-1930s, opening the Park to a different type of user as well as offering an alternate means of transport for the lumber industry. However, when the importance of the railway began to fade and service from the east was stopped in 1946, the great lodges, once thriving enterprises, fell silent and were eventually dismantled. By 1959 all service along this line, previously among the busiest in Canada, was discontinued and a glorious era came to an end. Now only scattered and often obscure clues are all that remain of those early days.

Although Algonquin continues to supply timber to the lumbering industry, it has become far more important as a playground for outdoor recreationists. Today Algonquin provides outstanding camping, canoeing, fishing and wildlife-viewing opportunities. Drive-in campgrounds are not only found along Highway 60, the major access to and the only road crossing the Park, but also at other access points. With over 1,500 Interior campsites along the 1,600 kilometres of established canoe routes and almost 200 kilometres of backpacking trails, a wilder, more private style of camping is also available. Fish, most notably speckled and lake trout, thrive in the clear, cold waters, and fishermen frequently depart with the proof to support their fantastic stories.

Algonquin is renowned for its sparkling lakes such as Tanamakoon.

For the explorer who simply appreciates a beautiful area Algonquin will not disappoint. Throughout the Park crystal lakes and winding rivers are fringed with rugged cliffs and fragrant conifers. After cool nights near summer's end, these low-lying areas are smothered with heavy mists. In autumn western slopes flame with vivid colour, and as this show begins to fade the golds of poplars and tamaracks reign supreme. Later, the sparkling snows of winter also create dramatic splendour. Year-round the Park exhibits ever-changing personae that are unrivalled in brilliance or mood.

Algonquin Provincial Park is a very special place. Although the park has felt the touch of man, its heart and soul have survived intact. Loons still serenade the setting sun and pines continue to whisper secrets to the wind. Today's explorer can enjoy the natural wonders of the present as well as marvel at artifacts from the past.

Welcome to Algonquin! May your visit provide you with a wealth of life-long memories.

EVERY SEASON BRINGS new and dramatic changes to Algonquin. Both the landscape and the wildlife undergo spectacular transformations in the course of a year. Many of the phenomena for which the Park is famous demonstrate seasonal peaks in either activity or occurrence. By knowing the times of the year in which specific events occur, one can better plan a trip to coincide with some of those particular highlights (or, in the case of biting insects, to avoid them).

Each month is broken into three periods — early, middle and late. You might find that the symbol for "fair" activity (-) is located at the first of the month, the symbol for a higher level of activity [(o) for "good"] in the middle of the month, and the symbol representing the highest level of activity [(x) for "high"] at the end of the month. This simply indicates that your best chance of encountering this animal or phenomenon lies at the end of the month as opposed to the beginning of it. Some of the more frequently sought animals are illustrated here. While many are active year-round, there are particular times when they may be more easily viewed (or, as with wolves, more readily heard). Further information on specific animal activity throughout the seasons is found in **OBSERVING WILDLIFE**.

Algonquin Park is a tremendous place to view wildflowers and other plants. An invaluable aid to learning what species are found in the Park is "The *Checklist of Vascular Plants of Algonquin Provincial Park* (Technical Bulletin No. 4)", available through The Friends of Algonquin (see **BOOKSTORES** in Chapter 5). Also available through The Friends is the inexpensive yet lavishly illustrated publication *Wildflowers of*

Algonquin Provincial Park. This great book breaks down the Park into discreet habitats and discusses the ecology of many of the typical flowers that inhabit them. Additionally, conducted outings and evening talks with wildflowers as the theme are offered as part of the summer interpretive program. (See **THE INTERPRETIVE PROGRAM** in Chapter 5.)

May is the best month for viewing woodland flowers such as painted trillium.

While the blooming period of Algonquin flowers starts in mid-April and extends right through until late September, there are certain peaks in the flowering cycle, depending on habitat. In West Side hardwood forests, the forest floor is covered with flowers from late April through to late May. Hepaticas, spring beauties, Dutchman's-breeches, and red trilliums paint the ground before the tree leaves open overhead and intercept the sunlight. Once the maples unfurl their leaves and shade cloaks the forest floor, only a few specialized flowers such as Indian pipe and spotted coralroot thrive.

A second wave of floral bloom occurs in summer along the highway edges and other open areas including bogs. In early summer, floating bog mats blaze with the pinks of sheep laurel and rose pogonia, and the yellow of the carnivorous bladderworts. Along the highway, mullein, chicory, ox-eye daisy, hawkweeds, birds-foot trefoil, and, later in the season, goldenrods and asters brighten up your drive.

The East Side of Algonquin harbours different species of wildflowers because of its sandy and dry nature. In season, all through the dominant pine forests you will find trailing arbutus, fringed polygala, and pink lady's-slipper. Along the flowing rivers purple-fringed orchids and cardinal-flowers can be quite common. A number of the flowers found on this side of Algonquin either occur in lesser number or are not found at all on the West Side of the Park.

Admire and photograph all the flowers you like, but keep in mind that picking them is strictly forbidden.

After the flowers lose their splendour, the Park experiences yet another blast of colour. This one, though, does not require any searching on your part to view. The hardwood forests on the West Side of Algonquin most years come alive by late September. The green chlorophyll in the leaves breaks down revealing a stunning array of colours hidden beneath its camouflage. While most colours are already present in the leaf, reds tend to be produced after the chlorophyll vanishes. Male red maples turn the deepest shade of that colour (females turn yellow). Sugar maples, the most abundant trees on the west side, display a variety of colours ranging from yellow through orange to red. The leaf colour, while apparent every year, does vary in intensity. Summer droughts, early frosts, and fall temperatures all play a role in the of the richness of the display. Generally, peak of the show occurs either in the last week of September or the first week of October.

Once the hues of the maples have faded, the fall colours are by no means finished. The poplars change a bit later, and their brilliant yellows liven the Park by mid-October. The viewing deck at the Visitor Centre offers sensational displays of these trees. As time passes, the red oaks come to life and their russet leaves adorn many hilltops, particularly on the East Side. Last but certainly not least, the tamaracks or larches put on their show. These bog-loving trees are the only conifers to lose their needles for the winter. But before they drop, the needles turn an intense yellow-orange. All through Algonquin, waterways blaze with the gold of October tamaracks.

If you wish to find out more precisely how the fall colours are developing in a given autumn, you can call the Park Information Number (705-633-5572) or check the Park website (www.algonquinpark.on.ca). However, don't inquire before the middle of September and certainly don't bother during the winter!

One feature of Algonquin not illustrated on the following chart is the aurora borealis, otherwise known as the Northern Lights. Because the Park is situated on a high dome with no interference from city lights, the night sky is beautifully dark, which offers excellent stargazing opportunities as well as periodic views of the spectacular Northern Lights. The bizarre shimmering, at times colourful lights of the aurora are caused by interactions between the Earth's magnetic field and pockets of intensified magnetism in the sun's atmosphere. The aurora can be seen virtually any time of the year. Quite frequently it appears as a dull glow in the northern sky, while at other times pulsating rays shoot into the night. On occasion vivid colours brighten the sky. Green is frequent, but red can also occur. In rare instances the colourful rays fill the entire sky in a cathedral effect, creating a mind-boggling display.

Key to Seasonal Chart

Code	Activity	Level of Activity	
1	Otter	-	Fair
2	Moose	o	Good
3	Wildflowers	x	High
4	Wolf Howling		
5	Beaver		
6	Biting Insects		
7	Fall Colours		
8	Ski / Snowshoe		

Seasonal Occurrences of a Few Algonquin Phenomena

	Jan	Feb	Mar	Apr	May	Jun	Jul	Aug	Sep	Oct	Nov	Dec
1	---	---	oox	xxx	o--	---	-oo	ooo	ooo	ooo	oo	---
2	---	---	oox	xxx	xxx	xxx	xxx	oo	ooo	ooo	ooo	---
3				-o	xxo	oox	xxx	oo	-	-		
4	ooo	ooo	ooo	o--	---	---	oxx	xxx	xxx	xxo	ooo	ooo
5				--o	xxx	xxx	xxx	xxx	xxx	xxx	xo-	
6				-	-ox	xxx	ooo	-				
7									-ox	xo-		
8	xxx	xxx	xo-									-ox

ALGONQUIN IS FAMOUS for its abundance and variety of wildlife, the result of the Park's mixture of southern and northern habitats. For many visitors the "must sees" include moose, Common Loons, beavers, Gray Jays, otters and wolves, although there is usually only a chance to hear the latter. Quite often Algonquin is the place where a person encounters these animals for the first time.

First-time visitors are sometimes concerned about the danger posed by animals. One frequently asked question is: "Are there any poisonous snakes in Algonquin Park?" Although Massasauga rattlesnakes, the only venomous reptiles in Ontario, are found west of the Park, unfortunately they are not known in Algonquin. I say un fortunately because it would be fantastic to have these rare and relatively harmless serpents as part of the fauna. The elevations that allow for the formation of boreal bogs are also responsible for the exclusion of many animals. Simply put, the Park is too cold for these fascinating, nonlethal reptiles.

As a rule, the wild animals that roam Algonquin are also harmless. Some people are concerned about black bears but these mammals are normally quite shy and very difficult to find. Wolves are almost impossible to see. But there have been rare exceptions where a bold individual of either species has turned up. When camping, by keeping your campsite free of food after meals and never having food in your tent, you virtually eliminate the possibility of having a bear disturb you at night. If you do ever encounter a bear or wolf that seems unafraid (believe me, the odds of this happening are extremely slim), scare it off by making loud noises and, if necessary, by throwing objects at it. Report the incident to a Park official. But please keep in mind that this is exceedingly unlikely to happen, and that the danger you face in driving to Algonquin is far greater, by light years, than any danger posed by the natural inhabitants of the Park.

Although you can encounter many of Algonquin's animals by driving the roads or walking the trails, there are a few "tricks" that will substantially increase your chances of finding them during your visit to the Park. Since each species is usually located in a specific habitat at a certain time of the year, knowing the animal's life history will certainly aid you in your efforts. I highly recommend that you obtain the Algonquin Park publications on wildlife before your visit. These are inexpensive and do an excellent job of discussing the animals in terms of habitat preference. The appendix **IMPORTANT PUBLICATIONS** will provide the titles of these publications.

WILDLIFE-VIEWING ETIQUETTE

Before I begin to offer advice on how to find some of the Park's wildlife, I feel that it is absolutely essential that a short treatise on wildlife-viewing etiquette be given. Far too often during the excitement of seeing a wild animal up close for the first time, or while trying to get the ultimate photograph, the viewer's impact on the animal is overlooked. Algonquin's animals, no matter how tame they might appear to be, are indeed *wild* animals. Not only might a lack of consideration for the animal cause it unnecessary stress, it may also endanger yourself. Despite the obliviously contented look on the moose gleaning salt from the roadside ditch, that 450-kilogram (1,000-pound) animal can easily crush your skull with one kick of its great hoof. The most important rule to follow is: *Give all animals respect.* If a moose seems absurdly tame, why bother risking your life by testing its approachability to the limit? I'm not trying to create the impression that these animals are dangerous and one should be wary of them. Normally they are non-aggressive. But how can we predict their behaviour if a crowd of 50 people begins to swarm around them? These creatures can certainly panic and might run through a group as easily as around it. If young are present, the mother might perceive a threat to her offspring and react instinctively. Bull moose can be downright ornery during their breeding season in the fall. So play it safe by playing it smart. A few simple rules to follow are:

1. Never approach a wild animal too closely. Although it is impossible to provide *the* proper viewing distance, a general rule might be to stay back at least 20 metres from the larger animals.
2. Never lure animals onto roads where they might be hit by a vehicle, thereby endangering not only the animal but also the occupants of the vehicle.
3. Never harass wildlife by repeatedly playing recordings of or imitating their sounds in an effort to keep them close by or to attract them. If you are trying to get an owl, Spruce Grouse, wolf or moose to react to a recording or imitation, play or call only a few times to get the animal's attention, then enjoy its response without further stimulation.
4. At night avoid shining powerful car-operated search beams into the eyes of animals. Some of these lights generate a tremendous glare that could damage the light-sensitive eyes of nocturnal animals.
5. Although feeding Gray Jays and chipmunks is acceptable, larger animals, particularly bears, should never be fed.
6. Do not disturb nesting birds, including loons. If these birds are repeatedly flushed off their nests, odds are that the nesting attempt will fail.
7. If you do encounter an unusually tame bear or wolf, frighten it off by making loud noises and then report the animal to a Park official.

When and How to See Wildlife

For most wildlife the time of day is very important. Dusk arouses nocturnal animals; dawn initiates a flurry of activity in diurnal animals. Thus, the best time to look for animals is generally either the two or three hours following sunrise or the hour or two preceding sunset. I prefer the period from the predawn glow to about two hours after sunrise. Not only is this one of the best times to see wildlife, but it is also one of the most beautiful times of day. On cool mornings the heat of the sun warms your cheeks and also seems to penetrate your soul. In late summer spectacular mists shroud the waterways and other low places. At this time of day you feel a special closeness to the Park, a sensation that is difficult to put into words. And when you return to your breakfast table, the coffee, bacon and eggs taste extra good.

Since the behaviour of animals changes throughout the seasons, learning a bit about them before your visit might increase your chances of encountering them. For example, contrary to popular thinking, the best way to locate beavers is not to watch for them cutting down trees. During the summer in Algonquin, water plants form an important part of a beaver's diet. Therefore, the animal can usually be found by either watching for a V (the shape of the wake formed by a swimming beaver) cutting across the water or by scanning for a blunt-shaped head sticking up among the water-lilies.

Often an area that encompasses the borders of several different habitats might produce the largest variety of animals. Excursions to the edges of beaver ponds, swamps or larger bogs at the optimal times of day may reap the greatest rewards. You can enhance your viewing opportunities with a few simple tricks. If you are looking for birds, an easily produced series of sounds is almost guaranteed to draw them in for better viewing. Try making the sound *shhhhh,* then add a *p* to the front while doing so. The resulting noise is known as "pishing" or "spishing." By repeating *pshhhhh* in a short series (i.e., *pshhhhh, pshhhhh, pshhhhh, pshhhhh*), you should achieve amazing results. This call resembles the alarm calls of small birds and elicits a "mobbing" response in birds that hear it. Try "pishing" in quiet spots on trails or near forest edges. One word of warning, however. People who encounter you making that noise will inevitably be curious and yell, "What are you doing?" Never shout back, "Just pishing," or you might be misunderstood!

Another call that attracts larger birds, particularly hunters like owls or hawks, also serves to attract mammalian predators such as foxes, weasels (including martens and fishers), and occasionally even wolves. The sound is a squeal produced by noisily sucking on the knuckles of your index and middle fingers of one hand. When I lick my knuckles first, I find I achieve a better squeal. The resulting noise is similar to that of an injured prey and tends to draw the hunters in like steel to a magnet. Don't expect results every time, however. For this call to work the animal must be within earshot and must not have been alarmed by your presence.

Imitations of specific animal sounds will frequently entice the animals to respond and occasionally even appear. Perhaps the easiest animal to imitate is the Algonquin wolf, and nothing is more rewarding than to be under a star-studded sky and have a wolf's spine-tingling howl shatter the silence in response to your rendition of its call. Because a human howl has the exact same qualities as that of a wild wolf, Algonquin wolves readily answer a human imitation. Try giving a long howl that rises in the middle and drops at the end. Wait 10 to 15 seconds after an attempt before repeating it. I have found that if wolves respond it is usually after the second attempt. Sometimes, however, it takes several individual howls followed by a number of "group howls" (where one energetic person or two or three people simulate a pack by giving several consecutive howls each). An excellent explanation of howling is given in Algonquin Park

Algonquin wolves frequently howl in response to human imitations of their wild sounds.

Technical Bulletin No. 3, *Wolf Howling in Algonquin Provincial Park*, and superb recordings of wolves can be heard on the cassette *Voices of Algonquin*.

Wolves will answer all day, so try howling anytime, particularly if you find fresh tracks or droppings, especially those that are still steaming! At night, however, sounds carry better, and with less bird, wind, leaf and traffic noise, distant sounds are more easily discerned. Large openings such as creeks, lake edges and bogs provide better long-range transmission of sound and are usually the best places to try.

Barred Owls are common throughout the Park and can often be stimulated into calling by imitations of their booming "who cooks for you, who cooks for you aaawwwll." Other loud noises, including wolf howls, may also elicit a response. *Voices of Algonquin* has superb recordings of this bird. It is noteworthy that imitations or tapes of this call in daytime attract a

PLATE 1
Tracks and Scats of Algonquin Large Mammals

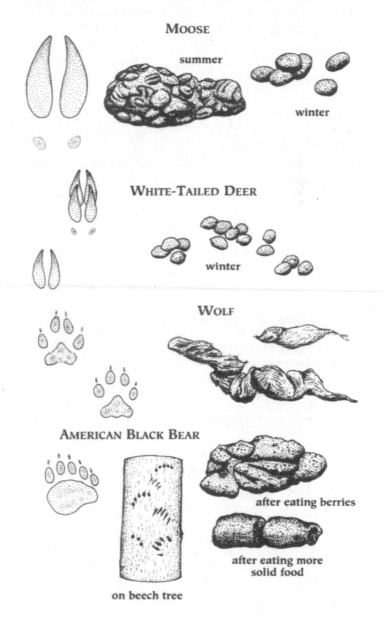

MOOSE
summer

winter

WHITE-TAILED DEER
winter

WOLF

AMERICAN BLACK BEAR
after eating berries

after eating more
solid food

on beech tree

variety of birds, particularly woodpeckers such as Yellow-bellied Sapsuckers, Northern Flickers, and the much sought after Black-backed Woodpecker. Before using a cassette, please read the section **WILDLIFE-VIEWING ETIQUETTE** in this chapter.

Otters are often seen on waterways throughout the Park. Frequently they respond to a snort and approach more closely. By blowing air through your mouth with your lips loosely flapping, an excellent rendition of an otter alarm call is produced. This sound will usually pique their curiosity and draw them in for better viewing.

The tremendous opportunity to view wild animals is indisputably one of the special features of Algonquin Park. Whether it be a chipmunk dominating a campground meal or a wolf howling into the night, these animals epitomize the untamed milieu for which the Park is famous. Please ensure that your enjoyment of these creatures does not have a detrimental effect either on them or on Algonquin.

GENERAL CAMPING

This Section is designed to provide a few basic camping tips. Bill Mason's *Song of the Paddle* is an excellent reference for more detailed camping information.

Camping Etiquette

Algonquin is becoming an increasingly popular place for visitors to explore. Unfortunately there are always a few campers who are inconsiderate slobs by nature and tend to leave campsites, portages and trails in unsightly messes. This kind of user is virtually impossible to educate. However, sometimes an unthinking act is performed simply out of ignorance. It is these unconscious acts that might be reduced with a little bit of camping etiquette. Some general rules to follow are:

1. Never cut down live trees for firewood. Sufficient wood can always be gathered from fallen branches or dead trees. In the public campgrounds wood can be purchased. You can also bring your own supply to the drive-in campsites.
2. Use the provided facilities at campgrounds or campsites for your "washroom deposits." If you are in dire straits (for example, the "mood" strikes while on a trail or portage), then make sure you go off the trail and scrape a shallow depression into the ground. After completion of your duties, cover up all evidence with soil and leaves.
3. Never leave garbage at a site, thinking that someone else will pack it out for you. Pack out all items not burnable. And remember, cans and bottles are prohibited in the Park Interior.

4. Use biodegradable soaps and shampoos on camping trips.
5. Never wash your dishes in lakes or rivers. Do this away from the water's edge.
6. Since sound travels so well at night, think of other campers when you feel moved to strike up a loud conversation or play a musical instrument. Be aware that radios, tape players and portable generators are not allowed in the Park Interior.
7. If possible, if you do encounter someone else's trash and you have room in your pack for it, consider carrying it out, as well.
8. Never start a fire outside of a designated fire pit and never leave a fire burning unattended.

Choosing a Site

Although camping in Algonquin can be broken down into two basic types, drive-in and Interior, there are site choices available for each. Along Highway 60 the campgrounds vary tremendously in available facilities as well as general environment. Too often a person grabs the first open campsite only to discover that another choice may have been preferable. If you are using a tent, never set it up in a depression. It can and certainly does rain in Algonquin, and low sites (as are frequently found in Lake of Two Rivers Campground) may fill up with water after a heavy rain. When choosing a site for a tent, try to select a slightly elevated, level area. If rain is anticipated, a heel-dug trench around the tent may help direct surface water away.

When tripping in the Interior, island campsites are preferred for a couple of reasons. As a rule, there is more wind and therefore fewer problems with biting insects. Also, islands frequently offer enhanced aesthetics in terms of sunrise and sunset viewing.

Remember, Interior camping may only be done at designated sites.

Algonquin offers superb wilderness camping experiences.

Equipment

Since an excellent treatment of camping equipment is covered in specific books, such as Bill Mason's *Song of the Paddle*, only a few tips are offered here.

A portable camp stove is a must for any camping trip. For drive-in camping larger multi-burner stoves with big fuel tanks are commonly used. For Interior trips smaller single-burner backpacking stoves are preferred. The Coleman Peak series, MSR Whisperlite and Optimus stoves are a few examples. Remember that a camp stove is essential for any backpacking or canoeing trip, not only because of potential bad weather but also due to possible fire bans in the drier summer season.

For Interior camping no trip is complete without a good length of rope, toilet paper, a flashlight with new batteries, a first-aid kit, waterproof matches and either a *Canoe Routes of Algonquin Provincial Park* or a *Backpacking Trails of Algonquin Provincial Park* map brochure.

Ziploc bags seem to have been invented for Interior tripping, since they can be used to keep maps, toilet paper and food dry. Although waterproof matches can be purchased, I still place these (along with their striking pad) and regular strike-anywhere matches in airtight containers. Formerly I used 35 mm film canisters for holding matches and spices (it has been suggested that chemical residue from the film may be unhealthy) but have now discovered a far superior container — urine-sample bottles, the kind common in medical clinics, are great for camping trips: they are extremely lightweight and also very waterproof. In case you are wondering, I only use new bottles.

Even though a light camping axe can be a useful piece of equipment, I often go on shorter trips without one. A folding saw, such as a Sven, is lighter to pack, occupies less space than an axe and is also more practical. Since the bulk of firewood used is generally branch-sized, the saw is all you need to cut up wood. For more extended trips I pack both a saw and an axe. After a day or two of hard rain, much of the smaller wood gets soaked, so I use my saw to cut up small blocks from larger fallen trunks, then split them with the axe to get at the drier wood inside.

When on an Interior trip, one very important rule is to keep matches and your sleeping bag free of moisture. While many of the sleeping bag sacks are reasonably waterproof, I still put my sleeping bag in a garbage bag to ensure dryness.

The One-match Fire

Whether you are camping in a public campground along the highway or on a remote island reached after a day's paddle by canoe, the mechanics of successfully starting a campfire are the same. Too often an attempt is made to ignite chunks of wood the size of a tree trunk. The best strategy is to start small and only add larger pieces of wood after the fire is established. In fact, many cooking fires only require wood the thickness of a pencil.

Fires must be set only inside the pit located at every designated camping spot. If the pit is full of loose ash from previous fires, clean it out before you prepare your fuel. Prior to constructing your fire, make sure that adequate fuel has been collected. If you are in a public campground, wood is sold at designated places and times. *Never* cut down living trees or strip bark or branches from them. Even the most heavily used Interior sites will have sufficient starting fuel near the fire pit.

Start off with a base of loose, easily ignited material. If you have waste paper with you, that will suffice. I find that small strips of white birch bark, which can usually be found lying on the ground or can be taken from logs or dead trees, works extremely well. If neither is available, dry pine needles and/or knife shavings from a dry stick will do. Next, add fine twigs, or "twiglets," as I call them. The best kind to use are the very fine dead twigs found on the bottom branches of coniferous trees such as spruce and balsam fir. These are also usually scattered on the ground. If you are in a campground, use an axe to slice off thin slivers of wood, otherwise known as "kindling." A couple of handfuls should be enough. On top of this add larger twigs and small branches (or larger kindling if at a campground), forming a rough pyramid. Now strike a match and light the base. Unless you are making an evening's-end fire, the largest wood pieces required should be the same size as the last ones you added to this fuel pile.

If a strong wind is blowing, build a windbreak out of stones. A strategically placed backpack will also help reduce the effect of the breeze. Never build a large fire under windy conditions. The camp stove should be used when cooking under these conditions.

When it comes time to call it a day, be sure to put out your fire. While it may be calm when you retire to the tent, a wind could easily spring up overnight. Also, never leave a site while a fire is still burning or the coals are still glowing, and thoroughly dowse the pit with water to ensure no accidents happen.

Wood can be purchased at the drive-in campgrounds, but there is nothing wrong with bringing your own supply.

Food

Perhaps the most important rule is never to have a messy campsite. Food scraps, dirty dishes, exposed food and even coolers left lying around serve to attract a variety of animals, including black bears and raccoons. If you are staying in a drive-in campground, place all waste material in the bearproof garbage structures. Never bring food into your tent; the odours will linger, possibly attracting a hungry scavenger. Make sure food is not left on the tables and that coolers are stored in your vehicle trunk overnight or when you are away from the site. If you are staying at an Interior site, burn all burnable leftovers and place nonburnables with your food in a pack hung well off the ground.

I usually bring at least one 10-metre rope on all Interior trips. Pines with a stout lower limb projecting from the trunk at least four metres above the ground are ideal for hanging packs. If you have difficulty throwing the rope over a branch, try weighting it with a piece of wood or a stone.

Sometimes two ropes are necessary if a suitable tree can't be found. You can tie one length between two adjacent trees, then hang the other piece over the first one. However, single trees are far simpler for hanging packs, and a bit of searching near the site will usually turn one up.

The pack should be hung at least three metres (nine feet) off the ground and at least one metre (three feet) from the trunk. *Never* leave your food in a pack on the ground, in the canoe or in the tent overnight or when you are away from the campsite.

The type of food a person brings to the Park depends primarily on the type of camping one does. Drive-in campgrounds allow the visitor to bring virtually any type of food. Canoeists and backpackers must carry lighter and less easily spoiled foods, but no cans or bottles. Excellent suggestions for suitable foods to bring can be found on the back of the *Canoe Routes of Algonquin Provincial Park* map brochure, the essential publication for any Park canoe trip, and Bill Mason's *Song of the Paddle*.

When walking trails exceeding two kilometres in length, it may be wise to bring food and beverages to get you through the trip.

Water

Drive-in campgrounds have treated water available. For Interior trips water must be used from untreated sources. Many users, including myself, drink water from larger lakes untreated. This practice is generally safe if water is taken away from the shore and down as far as the hand can reach. However, there is always a remote chance of contacting giardia or "beaver fever" by drinking untreated water, so many campers use either filtration systems or purification tablets available at any camping or outfitting store.

Boiling the water will also make it potable but, unfortunately, if you want a cool drink, you have to wait quite a while. Backpackers should carry water with them, replenishing reserves if necessary when lakes are encountered. Regardless of where you are in the Park, never drink untreated water from beaver ponds or bogs.

Clothing

Because of Algonquin's elevations the nights can be surprisingly cool, even cold, in late spring and midsummer. The best strategy if you are camping in drive-in locations is to bring a heavy sweater or jacket, perhaps even a light parka, especially in August. If you are camping in the Interior, then several layers of clothes are preferable to a heavy parka. Layers of loose clothes tend to be warmer (each layer traps air) than one heavy garment. A T-shirt, a long-sleeved cotton shirt, a light sweater and a windbreaker should do quite nicely. The beauty of layering is that you can mix and match to suit the temperatures. Be sure to bring rainwear no matter where or when you are camping, otherwise you may be confined to either wearing wet clothes or staying inside the tent until the rain ends, which might be several days. One important consideration is colour. During fly season (see **Biting Insects** in this chapter), light colours such as tan or pale yellow are much better than dark colours, especially blue or black.

Footwear should consist of shoes with good treads for walking trails or portages. Although hiking boots might seem ideal for Algonquin, as far as most people are concerned, including myself, they are not necessary. Comfortable hiking shoes or good running shoes normally suffice. The important thing is to bring a spare pair in case one pair gets wet. If you have weak ankles and are concerned about sprains, then hiking boots might offer better support. However, travelling along an Algonquin trail is not like climbing the Rocky Mountains, although the Centennial Ridges Trail might be the exception!

OTHER TIPS

The following will cover a few more general pieces of advice for Park users.

Biting Insects

The main challenge when camping in Algonquin at certain times of the year is dealing with biting insects. The good news is that each insect has its own particular season. The bad news is that the seasons tend to merge, producing a prolonged period of bloodletting. However, different people respond to each type of insect differently, and there are ways of reducing your attractiveness to these biting terrors.

First, let's meet the little devils. Black flies are among the smaller biting flies in Algonquin. Since they lay their eggs on rocks in fast-flowing, cold streams, Algonquin is perfect for a number of species to call "home". The majority of those that bite emerge as adults from these cold waters in spring, usually anywhere from mid-May to mid-June. However, during an early spring they might venture out in late April, and some years they persist well into July.

For those who have never met the black fly, you will be amazed at how such a tiny creature can make life so miserable. Black flies are active on warm days, particularly in the evening, but desist when the sun sets. Like most biting flies, it is only the female that bites, seeking a blood meal for her developing eggs. However, black flies tend to tear rather than bite flesh. Blood, induced by anticoagulants injected into the wounds, copiously flows from the small gashes. just like sharks drawn to a bloodbath, seeming thousands soon attack in a relentless and furious feeding frenzy.

Mosquitoes are the next most common type of biting insect in Algonquin. Although these creatures have a much longer flying season than black flies (they tend to appear by late May and some species remain active into the middle of August), they are rarely as bothersome as their smaller brethren. Of course, this is all very subjective; some people find a couple of mosquitoes totally unbearable. Mosquitoes tend to dominate the last hour or so of the day but can also be encountered while prowling around moist woods. Any portage through rich hardwoods or low areas will inevitably produce a hungry swarm.

By midsummer another "nasty" creature appears. Deer flies are larger flies with banded wings and gorgeous eyes (usually red or green). Their most common point of attack is your head, which they love to buzz around. Horse flies are a larger relative of deer flies. Both types of flies impart a nasty burning prick when they "let you have it."

One last type of fly that you might encounter in summer, particularly along waterways, is the stable fly. These house-fly-sized insects have the annoying habit of biting your ankles when you are canoeing and are very adept at escaping your swat no matter how fast you might be.

With all that said what can possibly be done apart from visiting the Park at another time of year, say, December? Well, there are actually a few things you can do to lessen the annoyance these small but at times dominant animals might cause you.

A number of effective insect repellents are available on the market. Since biting insects tend to home in on water vapour gradients next to your skin, the drying effects of these repellents tend to disrupt the insect's detection systems. Many types contain the active ingredient DEET. While these repellents work quite well for many people, I can't tell you which types work the best for the simple reason that I don't use them. I dislike the "meltdown" effect most brands have on binoculars and camera equipment. Some types lack DEET in their constitution and have components such as citronella instead. These may be an alternative for those who find the first chemical unpleasant.

Clothing selection is certainly important in insect avoidance. Many biting insects are attracted to dark colours, particularly dark blue and black. Lighter colours such as pale yellow or light tan will help you avoid the biting clouds. I will never forget paddling by a campsite one evening in early June. On the point stood a forlorn-looking woman, dressed in black pants and a black top and sporting a black hat. This was at the height of the black fly season, and her face and neck were a mass of open bleeding wounds from the fly bites. Although I wasn't enjoying the company of the flies swarming around me, I only bore a couple of bites on my exposed flesh.

Besides being light in colour, clothing should be loose-fitting with tight cuffs. I close all buttons and raise the collar. Usually I wear a light-coloured jacket over the shirt. A hat is essential to keep the pests out of your hair. Flies love tender ankles for dessert, so a pair of heavier socks pulled over your pant legs will protect these body parts. I must admit this sort of outfit tends to look silly, but believe me, in Algonquin during the height of fly season, fashion-wise clothes are as useless as high heels on the Centennial Ridges Trail.

Another trick I find to be quite successful is one that is also a little embarrassing to share with you. Perfumes in soaps and shampoos seem to attract insects, as do open pores from frequent bathing. If I am camping or taking photographs during peak fly season, I tend to bathe very irregularly. When I absolutely must clean myself, I avoid using soap of any type. There is a definite inverse relationship between the number of flies that bite you and the number of days since your last bath. Also, I wear the same clothes for as long as possible without washing them. Although these are excellent ways of reducing the number of biting flies, you won't win any friends.

Last but not least there are some excellent bugproof clothes on the market, including the traditional netted "bug hat," which might make you look like something from outer space. Then there are "bug jackets" that keep insects away from your body. Some of these must be dipped in the noxious repellents before they work. However, one type sold by most outfitters is an exception. Its elasticized cuffs and drawstring waist protect you from insects. The hood has a mesh face guard and can be unzipped at the neck to free your head. The best one I have tried is the Original Bug Shirt, which is made of lightweight tan cotton and has vents to prevent sweating. In the ultimate test I sat next to a beaver pond at the height of black fly season for several hours in the evening with this jacket on. I was amazed that none of the 2,989 black flies swarming outside this barrier were able to get in. I was also pleased that I could see well enough through the mesh to focus my camera without unfastening the hood.

Whatever method you use to combat biting insects there are always some inherent drawbacks. However, you will find the more you expose yourself to insects the less bothersome they are. If you are severely affected by their bites, as some people are, I would recommend that you come to Algonquin during the off-season for flies. Usually

Centennial Ridges Trail offers some of the most spectacular vistas in the Park.

the period from mid-August to late September is free of these insects, and at this time the temperatures are quite pleasant for sleeping in a tent.

Poisonous Snakes, Mushrooms and Poison Ivy

Campers are frequently concerned about poisonous plants and animals. Once again, there are no poisonous snakes in Algonquin. There has been but one lonely patch of poison ivy found along the Highway Corridor, just west of the Tea Lake Campground, although immature sarsaparilla plants are often mistaken for this species. On the other hand, poison ivy is occasionally encountered north of the Corridor and is relatively common along rivers in the eastern part of the Park.

There are a few poisonous mushrooms so, unless you are quite familiar with this type of fungi, avoid eating any during your visit. *Mushrooms of Algonquin Provincial*

Park is an excellent publication for those seeking more information.

Walking the Trails

Since most of the interpretive trails are short, no special advice is needed for them. However, some of the trails, notably Mizzy Lake, Track and Tower and Centennial Ridges, are longer and require more time to complete. To avoid running into difficulty I recommend starting the trail early in the morning as opposed to late afternoon. If you are inclined to start a longer trail later in the day, bring a flashlight.

It is also prudent to carry a small daypack with a bit of nourishment, such as trail mix or fruit, and some type of beverage in a container that will return with you. It can get quite hot in summer, and on most of the longer trails you will come across a few hills.

It is always an excellent idea to bring along some toilet paper or Kleenex. One never knows when "nature will call." Be sure to be discreet. Walk well off the trail, deposit "the goods" in a depression and cover up the "dirty deed" with leaves and soil once you are finished. Dogs are allowed on all trails except Mizzy Lake but must be kept on a leash, as is the rule all through Algonquin Park. Please bag "doggie deposits" and dispose appropriately.

Hunting in Algonquin

At present, hunting occurs in two parts of Algonquin. In the southern townships of Clyde, Bruton, and Eyre, deer and moose hunting occurs in the fall, as does the hunting of other game species. Members of the Algonquin First Nation are also permitted to hunt through approximately the eastern half of the Park, from mid-October (after Canadian Thanksgiving) through to mid-January or until their quota is met. There are restrictions concerning where hunting is allowed in these regions. For more information on this topic contact Algonquin Park (see Information Services under **IMPORTANT ADDRESSES AND PHONE NUMBERS** in Appendix 1)

Plate 2
Some Common Algonquin Conifers

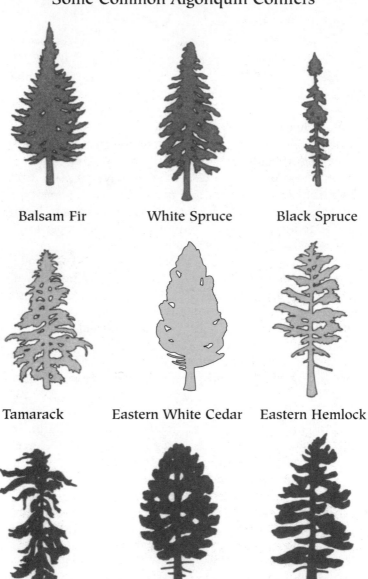

Balsam Fir   White Spruce   Black Spruce

Tamarack   Eastern White Cedar   Eastern Hemlock

Jack Pine   Red Pine   White Pine

PLATE 3
Leaves of Select Algonquin Deciduous Trees

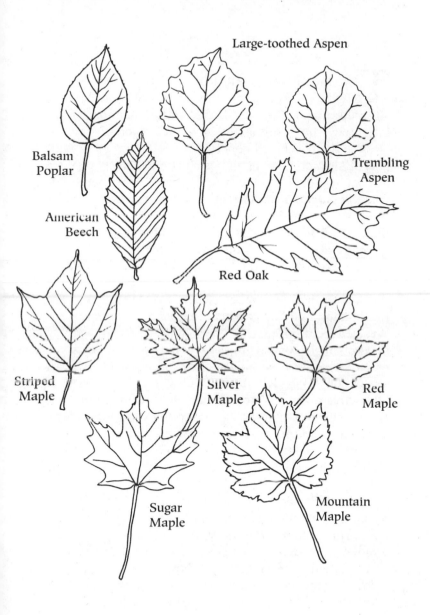

Large-toothed Aspen

Balsam
Poplar

American
Beech

Trembling
Aspen

Red Oak

Striped
Maple

Silver
Maple

Red
Maple

Sugar
Maple

Mountain
Maple

THE MOST POPULAR ROUTE into Algonquin is Highway 60. Along the Highway Corridor are situated the majority of the Park's campgrounds, interpretive trails and facilities, as well as other services. Despite the developed aspect and prominent use of this part of Algonquin, it is still possible to feel as though you are really "back in the woods" and have bona fide wilderness experiences. Also, wildlife-viewing opportunities in the Corridor are equal to, in some cases better than, those off the road in the Park Interior.

Information and permits, which every vehicle must display, are available at both the East and West gates. The East Gate is easily located because you must pass through a set of arches when you reach it. The Information Building is accessed from the right lane. The West Gate entrance has been modified in recent years so that you might conceivably pass it if distracted. After you reach the western boundary of Algonquin (identified by a sign on your right side), the West Gate lies four kilometres ahead. Watch for the right-turning lane that enters the parking area adjacent to the West Gate office. Remember, you must have a permit whether you are in the Park for a half day or a week. Only people just passing through the Park (i.e., not using Park facilities) are not required to buy a permit.

Reflective signs, frequently situated on telephone posts, indicate the distance in kilometres from the West Gate. Throughout the Park literature locations of points of interest are defined using these kilometre markers.

For example, the Western Uplands Backpacking Trail is located three kilometres east of the West Gate at the kilometre 3 (KM 3) sign, and the road to the Algonquin

The Highway 60 Corridor is one of the most popular access points.

Visitor Centre lies at the KM 43 marker, 43 kilometres east of the West Gate. The same system will be used in this book when describing locations along the Corridor. The distance between markers will be used for more precise location descriptions. For example, the Mizzy Lake Trail entrance is situated 0.4 kilometre east of the kilometre 15 (KM 15) marker. Thus, its location would be given as KM 15.4.

As you reach the Park Boundaries, you will see signs notifying you of the Park Information radio channel. By tuning in to CFOA at FM 102.7 on your car radio, you will receive a brief overview of current Park services and highway phenomena.

An excellent summary of the current Corridor facilities and activities can be found in the free tabloid *Algonquin Provincial Park: The Parkway Corridor*, available at most Park offices or upon request by mail or phone.

THE ALGONQUIN VISITOR CENTRE — KM 43

A major project undertaken for the Park centennial in 1993, the Algonquin Visitor Centre is without question one of the finest interpretive centres in Canada. Every aspect of this incredible showpiece, including the breathtaking location, is simply spectacular.

The first section of the display area illustrates how the Park's topography has affected the present-day composition of flora and fauna by its influence on climate and soils. The next gallery depicts through stunning dioramas all of the Park's major habitats, from spruce bog to hardwood forest, from lake to coniferous forest. The array of animals in the dioramas ranges from tiny shrews to massive moose. The animals are situated in realistic surroundings with painted backdrops that can only be described as genuine works of art. Whether it be the beaver pond diorama complete with dam, pond and lodge, or the bear exhibit with a mother bear tearing apart a log while her two cubs look on with curiosity, the realism is incredible.

The human history level profiles man's involvement in Algonquin. Exhibits profile various people, ranging from early inhabitants to more recent residents, such as the famous artist Tom Thomson, and discuss their involvement and impact on the Park. A comfortable theatre offers programs that further explain the past and present features of Algonquin.

The dioramas, displays and programs have all been designed to provide visitors with an understanding of the complexity of the Park. Visitors are now better prepared to appreciate the "real thing," which is gloriously on display from a partially enclosed viewing deck. The deck overlooks a spectacular vista encompassing a sweeping bog, rolling hardwood hills, two lakes and a boreal forest — the very subjects explained throughout the displays inside. The view alone is worth the trip. Occasionally animals such as moose, bears and wolves are seen or heard from this wonderful vantage point.

The Algonquin Visitor Centre offers a spectacular view.

The Visitor Centre also contains a restaurant an information desk and an excellent bookstore, as well as a room for temporary exhibits. The Centre is open seven days a week for most of the year (in winter it may be open only weekends). Be sure to set aside at the very least a part of a day to visit this outstanding facility.

THE ALGONQUIN LOGGING MUSEUM — KM 54.6

This outdoor museum offers a fascinating look at an important aspect of Algonquin's history. The log Reception Building houses an information desk, a bookstore, a theatre and dioramas that depict logging activities. An audiovisual program provides an overview of the logging history of the Park, and a delightful trail complete with guidebook starts from the Reception Building and leads through the outdoor exhibits. These

37

include a replica of an early camboose camp and one of the last remaining alligators, a steam-driven paddle boat that could also be winched across land. Around the turn of the century it was used for towing log booms. Appropriately this unique exhibit rests beside a scenic pond created by a replicated log dam. A log chute, similar to the ones used to transport logs around waterfalls and rapids, bypasses the small rapids below the dam.

The outdoor exhibits are strategically located along this trail in a chronological sequence, which allows the visitor to see how logging has changed over the past 150 years. The Algonquin Logging Museum is open from late May until Thanksgiving weekend.

THE ALGONQUIN GALLERY — KM 20

The Algonquin Gallery is well worth a visit during your stay in the Park. While long-time Park enthusiasts may recognize the outside of the building from its old Park Museum days, the inside has gone through a dramatic metamorphosis. Some of the Canada's finest wildlife art exhibitions are now held in the Gallery, which is open from late June through October. Works by famed landscape artists such as Tom Thomson and contemporary wildlife artists, including Robert Bateman, are exhibited in the Gallery. Refreshments and light meals are available at the Gallery Café, situated outside the Algonquin Gallery. Please note there is a fee to enter the Gallery. For information on current exhibits and prices call 1-800-989-6540 or, during the operating season, call the Gallery at 705-633-5225.

THE INTERPRETIVE WALKING TRAILS

One of the most appealing features of the Highway 60 Corridor is the variety of superb interpretive walking trails. There are 13 distinctly different trails, each offering unique insights into the Park's habitats and intriguing history. An inexpensive (37 cents in 1999!) illustrated trail guide is available at the start of each trail or at retail outlets in the Park. These booklets contain text that is read at corresponding numbered posts along the trail, allowing you to learn firsthand and at your own leisure about Algonquin's many facets.

The following is a brief synopsis of the different trails. The highway location follows the name of the trail. A brief overview of the trail is then provided and the trail length appears in brackets at the end of the description.

Whiskey Rapids Trail — KM 7.2

This trail follows the scenic Oxtongue River, and the trail guide explores the ecology of the river (2.1 kilometres).

Hardwood Lookout Trail — KM 13.8

This short trail brings you through a beautiful hardwood forest, while the trail guide explores its ecology. Scenic views of the Smoke Lake area and a side trail to a stand of red spruce, a relatively rare tree, are highlights (0.8 kilometre).

Mizzy Lake Trail — KM 15.4

This, the second longest trail, is well worth the effort because it passes through some outstanding wildlife-viewing areas, particularly in the northern part. A total of nine small lakes and ponds are visited, and the wildlife they support is highlighted in the trail guide. Please note that dogs are not allowed on this trail (11 kilometres).

Peck Lake Trail — KM 19.2

The ecology of very pretty Peck Lake is the focus of this trail, which meanders around the lake periphery through a delightful coniferous forest (1.9 kilometres).

Track and Tower Trail — KM 25

This popular trail explores some of the fascinating history of Algonquin. It travels through some extensive hardwood forests and crosses many pretty streams. The historic landmarks include remnants of several OA & PS Railway trestles and the site of a former fire lookout tower with a spectacular view over Cache Lake. Part of the trail lies on the old railway bed of the OA & PS Railway. The Track and Tower Trail can also be reached from Mew Lake (7.7 kilometres with an optional 5.5-kilometre loop from Mew Lake Campground).

Hemlock Bluff Trail — KM 27.2

This trail first leads through a grove of towering hemlocks and later visits a cliff overlooking Jack Lake. Research in Algonquin is the topic examined in the trail guide (3.5 kilometres).

Bat Lake Trail — KM 30.8

This trail is relatively easy to walk despite its length. it passes through a younger mixed forest, enters an exceptionally large hemlock grove, traverses a bog and visits a fine lookout as well as a naturally acidified lake. The trail guide examines basic ecological principles (5.6 kilometres).

Two Rivers Trail — KM 31

A fine view from a cliff top is the highlight of this trail, which wanders through a younger Algonquin forest. The dynamics of forest change are explored (2.1 kilometres).

Centennial Ridges Trail — two kilometres south from KM 37.6

The newest of the Corridor trails, it gets its name from its year of opening — 1993, the Park centennial. It is the most rugged of all the highway trails, but the hike is worth the effort. Some of the finest views in the Park are found atop the two ridges the trail visits. The trail guide details contributions made by famous Park personalities (10 kilometres).

Lookout Trail — KM 39.7

One of the most spectacular of all the trails, Lookout Trail holds true to its name and visits a cliff offering a breathtaking view. The trail guide explores the geology of

Algonquin. On the rather steep climb to the top (which means a downhill walk on the return) one encounters interesting features, including a glacial erratic (a glacier-moved rock) as big as a mobile home (1.9 kilometres).

Booth's Rock Trail — 9 kilometres south from KM 40.3

Another spectacular view is offered from this trail, which also visits two small lakes. After visiting the ruins of the Barclay Estate, you return on the old railway bed. Man's impact on Algonquin is the theme of the trail guide (5.1 kilometres).

Spruce Bog Boardwalk — KM 42.5

This short trail is not only one of the most unique but also one of the easiest to walk. The fascinating ecology of a northern bog is explored as you travel through and over the Sunday Creek bog on boardwalks. Northern flora and fauna highlight this trail (1.5 kilometres).

Beaver Pond Trail — KM 45.2

One of my favourites, this trail visits two beaver ponds and allows you to explore the ecology of this common Park mammal. Certainly one of the better wildlife-viewing trails (2.0 kilometres).

BIKE TRAILS

The Minnesing Mountain Bike Trail, at KM 23, occupies the Minnesing Cross-country Ski Trail. The 23 kilometres of trail traverse a variety of terrain and offer varying degrees of physical challenge, some sections more so than others.

The Old Railway Bike Trail follows the abandoned rail bed of the OA & PS Railway from Mew Lake to Rock Lake. This 10 kilometre family biking trail can be accessed from the Mew Lake Airfield, the Pog Lake Campground, the Whitefish Mill Site, and Rock Lake.

BACKPACKING TRAILS

Two excellent backpacking trails can be reached from the Highway Corridor. While both offer loops that can be walked in one full day (if you are in good shape and are an accomplished hiker), these trails are primarily designed for overnight use. The regulations for the Interior apply to users of this trail. Refer to **OTHER ACCESS POINTS** for details on these rules.

Backpacking Trails of Algonquin Provincial Park provides detailed maps and information concerning these trails. It is available from The Friends of Algonquin Park (address provided in the appendix **IMPORTANT SERVICES**) or from the gates.

The Western Uplands Backpacking Trail — KM 3

This is the longest backpacking trail in the Park and offers loops ranging from 32 to 88 kilometres. Access to this trail is also achieved from the Rain Lake Access, providing backpackers with the option of hiking the trail from Highway 60 to Rain Lake, or vice versa, without returning. As its name suggests, this trail travels through typical West Side hardwood uplands.

Highland Backpacking Trail — KM 29.7

This trail offers loops of 19 and 35 kilometres. The short loop encircles Provoking Lake while the longer loop also visits Head and Harness lakes.

CROSS-COUNTRY SKI TRAILS

During winter Algonquin is enveloped by a silent beauty not found at other times of the year. Three excellent cross-country trails allow skiers to explore the Park during this invigorating season. All the trails have shelters (many with heat available) and emergency barrels (each containing a first-aid kit, spare ski tip, roll of duct tape, matches, fire starter, kindling, candies, an emergency blanket, sleeping bag and chocolate bars) at points along their lengths. Each trail is packed and groomed, and track-setting occurs whenever weather conditions and manpower permit. Various levels of challenge are offered and identified on each trail.

The free brochure *Algonquin Provincial Park in Winter* details these trails and supplies general winter regulations and tips. It is available at the park gates.

Fen Lake Trail — starts at West Gate

This trail offers loops of 1.25, 5.2 and 13 kilometres. Much of the trail passes through typical West Side hardwood forest.

Minnesing Trail — KM 23.2

The return section of the trail follows the historic Minnesing Road which, in early years, carried visitors from the railway station at Cache Lake to the Minnesing Lodge on Burnt Island Lake. A variety of loops, varying from 4.7 to 23.4 kilometres, offer skiers a number of options. The trail traverses a variety of terrain, and spectacular scenery is a feature over much of its length.

Leaf Lake Trail — KM 53.9

This is one of the favourite trails of Algonquin skiers. A large number of habitats and spectacular vistas are seen. Several loops allow for a variety of distances to be covered during the outing. Here one can ski as little as five or as many as 17 kilometres of trail.

Leaf Lake Horse Trail

This horse trail, one of only four in Algonquin (the others are the White Partridge Lake, the Lone Creek, and the Algonquin South horse trails), is open only from August through October. The entrance is 1 kilometre east of the East Gate and the trail in part follows the Leaf Lake Ski Trail. All Park regulations apply to trail users. More information can be obtained from Park Information Services (705-633-5572)

Dog Sled Trail

In recent years, a winter dog sled trail has been established. The parking area is on the north side of the highway, directly across from Rock Lake Road (km 40.3) Contact Park Information Services for details concerning the trail (705-633-5572).

PICNIC GROUNDS

Five picnic grounds are situated along the Corridor. In order of appearance from west to east these are Oxtongue River (KM 3), Tea Lake Dam (KM 8.1), Lake of Two Rivers (KM 33.8), Lake of Two Rivers East (KM 35.4) and Costello Creek (KM 46.3). While all are kept clean and have outdoor washrooms, there are several that are more aesthetically pleasing because they are situated on water. Perhaps the prettiest of all is the Tea Lake Dam Picnic Ground, found on the picturesque Oxtongue River. The Lake of Two Rivers sites are also quite nice thanks to their location on a large, scenic lake with good beaches within easy access of the picnic sites. In addition to these official picnic grounds, picnic tables are also located at Canisbay Lake (north from KM 23.1), at KM 23.3 (north side of the highway) and at the Lake of Two Rivers Store (KM 31.4).

RESTAURANTS AND LODGES

Meals can be purchased along the highway at several locations. Generally the restaurants don't open until May and are usually open until Thanksgiving, except for the Visitor Centre restaurant, which offers full meals all winter. It is best to check in advance if you visit in the off-season and wish to eat in Park facilities. Your needs and budget will be considerations when choosing a place to eat inside the Park. The three lodges that serve meals to the general public as well as to their guests tend to be considerably more expensive, since they offer more elaborate meals. You may wish to inquire about prices before committing yourself. Of course, numerous restaurants are situated outside the Park and are open year-round.

All three lodges offer accommodation throughout most of the usual visitation season. Dates of operation and prices can be acquired by phone or letter, and addresses are provided in the appendix IMPORTANT SERVICES.

- The Portage Store (KM 14.1) offers light meals and the restaurant overlooks Canoe Lake.
- Arrowhon Pines Lodge (eight kilometres north from KM 15.4) offers full-course meals. It is best to reserve by phone (705-633-5661/5662).
- Gallery Café (KM 20) offers light meals and snacks in an outdoor setting.
- Bartlett Lodge (on Cache Lake, south from KM 23.5) is accessible by water only (a boat will taxi you to the lodge) and offers full-course meals. It is best to reserve by phone (705-633-5543).
- Lake of Two Rivers Store (KM 31.4) has a restaurant specializing in take-out fast food, and it also has a small sit-down section.
- Killarney Lodge (KM 33.2) offers full meal services, but it may be best to phone in advance (705-633-5551).
- The Sunday Creek Café (KM 43) is situated inside the Algonquin Visitor Centre. This large restaurant offers not only light meals and snacks but a spectacular view from the dining area.

STORES

Three stores are situated along the Highway Corridor. The Portage Store on Canoe Lake (KM 14.1) has a souvenir shop adjoining the restaurant, and a complete outfitting store is situated on the lower level. This is the only location in the Park where gasoline is available. The Lake of Two Rivers Store (KM 31.4) offers a variety of groceries and personal essentials as well as souvenirs. The Opeongo Store (north from KM 46.3) is primarily an outfitting store but does offer a small selection of drinks and camping foods. Some souvenirs are also available here.

BOOKSTORES

A superb bookstore operated by a cooperating association, The Friends of Algonquin Park, is located at the Algonquin Visitor Centre (KM 43). Publications specifically dealing with the Park are sold here as well as an excellent selection of natural history, human history and children's books. A host of other products including posters, videos, clothing, post cards, and camera batteries are also sold.

The Friends also operate a smaller bookstore at the Algonquin Logging Museum (KM 54.6). In addition, all the stores in the Park offer a small selection of publications. Park publications are also available at both gates.

You can join The Friends of Algonquin Park for a small fee. In addition to indirectly supporting Park programs and publications with your membership fee, you also receive a 15% discount on most items sold by The Friends. See **IMPORTANT ADDRESSES** in Appendix 1 for the address and phone number of The Friends of Algonquin Park.

CAMPGROUNDS

Nine campgrounds are situated in the Corridor. These vary tremendously in size, atmosphere and facilities. Electrical outlets, showers, laundry facilities, flush toilets, and a good beach are available at Canisbay (KM 23.1), Mew Lake (KM 30.6), Lake of Two Rivers (KM 31.8), Pog Lake (KM 36.9), and Rock Lake (8 km south of KM 40.3) campgrounds. Kearney Lake Campground (KM 36.5) lacks electrical outlets, while Tea Lake (KM 11.4) and Coon Lake (6 km south of KM 40.3) campgrounds lack all of the aforementioned facilities. Tea Lake, Lake of Two Rivers and Rock Lake are the only campgrounds where motorboats with up to 20 horsepower motors are allowed on the lake. Lake of Two Rivers and Mew Lake are within easy walking distance of the Lake of Two Rivers Store, which means these campgrounds are more exposed to highway noise. The ninth campground, Whitefish Group Campground (in from KM 36.9) is available for organized groups on a reservation basis only.

In Canisbay Lake, Mew Lake, and Pog Lake campgrounds certain sites are designated dog-free and radio-free. In sites where dogs are permitted, leashes must be used, as is the regulation all through the Park.

Mew Lake Campground also offers Furnished Tents also called Yurts. These are eight-sided tent structures mounted on insulated wooden deck floors. They are furnished with two sets of bunks beds, chairs, table, propane barbecue, lights, and an electric heater for fall and winter. Dishes, pots, pans, and cutlery are provided from May to Thanksgiving (Canadian). The fee in 1999 was $55 per night, $350 per week. Yurts can be reserved through Ontario Parks Reservations by phone (1-888-ONT-PARK = 1-888-668-7275) or through the Reservation Web Site (www.OntarioParks.com).

If privacy is your main concern, then I recommend Canisbay as the best and Pog Lake second best. Canisbay is situated in a beautiful hardwood forest with relatively isolated sites. Pog Lake lies in a plantation-style pinewoods and has many waterfront sites. Both campgrounds have sections that are well distanced from highway noise. Rock Lake and Lake of Two Rivers have the least isolated campsites and may be noisier than other campgrounds during the busy period (mid-July to mid-August). Obviously the type of facilities available and the degree of privacy offered are important factors to consider when choosing a campground.

Firewood is sold at wood yards in Mew and Pog Lake campgrounds, and at the Rock Lake office. During fall and winter, wood is available at Mew Lake.

Canisbay has an additional feature that other campgrounds lack. Campsites situated at the north end of the lake can only be reached by canoe. These are known as "paddle-in sites" and offer users a taste of Interior camping.

All campgrounds are open by the middle of June; Tea Lake, Canisbay, Two Rivers, and Rock Lake are open earlier, while Mew Lake is open year round.

Each campground has its own pamphlet complete with map of the sites. All campgrounds have sites that can be reserved. Reservations are recommended for much of the summer season due to the popularity of the campgrounds. Reservations can be made directly at the campgrounds or by telephone, year-round, 24 hours a day, at Ontario Parks Reservations (1-888-ONT-PARK = 1-888-688-7275). There is also a Reservation Web Site (www.OntarioParks.com). Please note there is a fee for the reservation service.

THE INTERPRETIVE PROGRAM

Algonquin has one of the finest interpretive programs in North America. Programs, held daily from late June until Labour Day, consist of Conducted Walks as well as Children's and Evening Programs.

The Conducted Walks are usually a leisurely hour and a half long and focus on specific subjects such as birds, wildflowers, insects, mushrooms, trees and forest ecology. In addition, slightly longer outings explore wildlife habitats at special times of the day. Evening Walks visit excellent habitats for beaver, moose and otter. Night Walks explore the nocturnal activity along a quiet trail, and the wild calls of Barred Owls are frequently a highlight. Canoe Outings are half-day events that explore aquatic habitats as well as provide some canoe tripping tips.

Algonquin for Kids focuses on the younger audience and deals with topics ranging from reptiles and amphibians to animal defences. These programs are held at the Algonquin Visitor Centre.

Evening Programs are held every night at the Outdoor Theatre (KM 35.4). They usually last about an hour and a half and consist of two films and a slide presentation. Topics include birds, reptiles and amphibians, beavers, wolves, moose, lakes and fishing, wildflowers, Tom

Thomson and canoe tripping. In bad weather the programs are held inside the Visitor Centre.

Spirit Walks, are extremely popular events held on Monday evenings in July at the Algonquin Logging Museum (KM 54.6). Park staff dress in period costume and act out entertaining scenarios at various outdoor exhibits along the trail. Free tickets, available at the Algonquin Logging Museum and the Algonquin Visitor Centre several days prior to each Spirit Walk, are required for admission to the events.

Public Wolf Howls are held on Thursdays in August if wolves and weather permit. At these immensely popular events participants first attend a talk on wolves and wolf howling at the Outdoor Theatre. Then they are taken to a site where naturalists attempt to elicit responses from wild wolves by giving vocal imitations of their howls.

In recent years the interpretive program has been offered on weekends between Labour Day and Thanksgiving. Evening Programs are performed indoors, but walks are still held outdoors.

All of the locations, times and themes of the events are provided in the weekly flyer *This Week in Algonquin*. This is available in dispensers and posted on bulletin boards throughout the Park. A special autumn edition lists all the events when fall programming is available.

The naturalist staff, both seasonal and permanent, is of the highest calibre. They are always more than willing to answer any questions concerning the Park's flora, fauna or history. If you would like something identified or desire information on any particular aspect of Algonquin, feel free to inquire at the Visitor Centre.

WILDLIFE-VIEWING AREAS

Many of the interpretive trails and outings offer excellent opportunities to encounter some of the Park's famed wildlife. Perhaps the two finest trails for general wildlife viewing are Beaver Pond and Mizzy Lake. Each offers a mixture of habitats, including ponds supporting active beaver colonies and superb summer moose-feeding sites.

Wolves also frequent these areas in some years, particularly late summer. In fact, Wolf Howl Pond on the Mizzy Lake Trail is so named because Algonquin wolves are commonly heard howling from the boggy meadows at the northwest end of the pond. Otters are also frequently seen, particularly in the waterways along the Mizzy Trail.

If encountering wildlife is one of the goals of your trip, refer to Chapter 3 for tips and advice on general wildlife viewing. Many of the species can be attracted with specific calls and noises, and these are outlined in this section. In Chapter 3, **WILDLIFE-VIEWING ETIQUETTE** offers recommendations on how to avoid disturbing the animals while you are viewing them.

The Wildlife Sightings Board in the Visitor Centre (KM 40) is an excellent source of information on virtually all of the species you might be interested in seeing. Visitors record their sightings here daily.

The following is a discussion of sites for some of the more popular species. For simplicity the sites are listed from west to east.

Moose

In its earlier history, Algonquin Park was famous for its white-tailed deer population. While deer are still present in the Park, moose, their larger cousin, are now more regularly viewed, at least in this part of Algonquin. While an excursion by canoe into the Park Interior is an excellent way of meeting up with one of these giants, one can also encounter them right from the car almost anywhere in the Highway Corridor.

When I began to work in Algonquin in the early 1970s, there were probably only a few hundred moose present and to see even one in the entire summer was a thrill. By the mid-1980s their numbers had grown significantly, and by 1990 they numbered in the thousands. At that time you could encounter as many as two dozen moose in one pass of the highway between the Park Gates. There were few places better in the entire world for viewing moose.

However, the moose numbers gradually dropped through the 1990s. Part of the decline was possibly due to overcrowding pressures, which was reflected in a dramatic drop in the number of calves born in May. When the moose population was growing rapidly, up to 90% of the cows bore twins. By the early 1990s, that percentage dropped to the low teens. But the moose numbers also fell for another reason. In the winters of 1991–92 and 1998–99, many moose carried a heavy load of winter ticks, an external parasite that feeds on blood. By the early spring in both tick years, numbers of moose were found dead from hypothermia. In an effort to rid themselves of the annoying ticks the moose rub against trees and bite off their hair. This loss of the insulating coat exposes moose to the cold and some perish. In a one-week period in April 1999, a total of 24 moose were found dead just along Highway 60. But this seemingly high casualty rate must be put into perspective. Outbreaks of this nature are not common; in fact, their frequency in Algonquin Park appears to be a case of the seven-year itch!

Moose are easily viewed as they glean salt from spring roadsides.

Despite a lower birth rate and a higher winter mortality in some years, there are still plenty of moose to be seen in Algonquin, and the Park remains one of the best places for viewing them. Even though moose can be encountered all through the year, there are certain periods when they are more easily found. In particular, spring is a great time. During the winter, moose lack sodium, an essential mineral, in their diet. By spring, sodium starved moose that wander by the highway discover the roadside ditches are full of sodium originating from the salt used in winter road maintenance. Numbers of moose can be readily viewed from April through June in highway ditches, gleaning sodium from the puddles and wet mud.

From June through to late July moose get their natural source of sodium from water plants, especially watershield. A number of lakes, ponds and streams along the highway edge offer good viewing opportunities, particularly in the evening.

I recommend checking: the pond on the north side of the highway at KM 21.4 (there is a pull-off here); Eucalia Lake (KM 39); the pond on the south side of the highway at KM 40.8; the pond opposite the turn for the Opeongo Road (KM 46.3); and Costello Creek along the Opeongo Road north of where the creek crosses under the road (approximately 3 km north of the highway).

Perhaps the best two trails for viewing moose in summer are Mizzy Lake (KM 15.4, especially along the old railway bed, which forms the northeastern section of the trail) and Beaver Pond (KM 45.2). Watch for moose sign on these and most other Algonquin trails. Clumps of fibrous pellets the size of meat balls are winter droppings. Vertical scars on red maple (and striped maple) trunks at about eye level are usually the result of late winter bark feeding episodes. While it has been suggested that this behaviour is starvation induced, because the moose are very specific as to what tree bark they eat I suspect there is some other nutritional reason behind this phenomenon.

Although they might be encountered most places along the roadside, more moose are usually viewed east of the Algonquin Gallery (KM 20) than west of it. In addition to the sites discussed above some areas along the highway where frequent sightings have been made, particularly in early summer, include:

- Cache Lake region — KM 22.3 to KM 23.8.
- Track and Tower Trail region — KM 25.
- Hemlock Bluff Trail region — KM 27.2 to KM 27.6.
- Kearney Campground to Eucalia Lake — KM 36.5 to KM 39.
- Eos Lake to Beaver Pond Trail — KM 43.8 to KM 45.2.
- West Smith Lake to the Algonquin Logging Museum — KM 51.5 to KM 54.6.

Moose are at their magnificent best in September when their breeding season, the rut, begins. The plush skin that adorns the growing antlers of the bulls during summer has been shed, and the fully grown bone structures glow orange in the early morning light. By mid-September, the cow moose have begun to call for the bulls. During the night up till dawn (occasionally during the day), you can sometimes hear their loud nasal bawls right from the highway. Several areas over the years have proven good for moose during the rut. The Visitor Centre (KM 43) has provided many a visitor with good looks at moose through the telescopes on the viewing deck. The Opeongo Road has also been an excellent spot, especially near the culvert where Costello Creek flows under the road. This is my favourite location for looking for moose along the highway. While it has been good for seeing moose, this site also offers some of the most spectacular scenery in the Park. When early morning mists cloak the boggy creek, it is easy to forget that you are there to look for moose.

I must offer a word of warning, however, about moose at this time of year. The bulls can be ornery - I have been charged twice by bulls along this road and on other occasions elsewhere. Do give them plenty of space and do not try to follow them if they walk into the woods.

The Wildlife Sightings Board in the Visitor Centre will also provide you with good locations to check.

Algonquin Wolves

Originally it was believed that the wolves in Algonquin Park belonged to a small race of gray or timber wolf. Although they sound and behave like timber wolves farther north, Algonquin wolves have always been a bit of a puzzle for they are considerably smaller than northern wolves {the average male weighs in at 28 kilograms (61 pounds)} and they are coloured quite differently. With little variability through the entire population (as high as 300 when the pups are born in spring), Algonquin wolves are gray and black with rust-coloured ears, snouts, and flanks. Then, in the late 1990s, DNA research by Dr. Brad White of McMaster University in Ontario shed some light on the picture. The DNA analysis revealed that Algonquin wolves were genetically much more closely affiliated with the red wolf, an endangered species of wolf residing in the southeastern United States, than they are with gray wolves. It also revealed that Algonquin wolves and coyotes are more closely related to each other than to gray wolves found through much of Canada, Alaska, and a few areas in the northern United States. This led Dr. White to hypothesize that Algonquin wolves and red wolves are one and the same, and that their quite disjunct populations are a result of the colonization of eastern North America. The gray wolves, in this new theory, are relative new-comers to North America, arriving (likely with the moose) when a land bridge formed between Alaska and the Siberia during the time of the glaciers. At the time of writing, more work is being done on this exciting find. Current information and exhibits on Algonquin wolves can be found in the Algonquin Visitor Centre.

Although one of the most difficult to see of all of Algonquin's large animals, at certain times of the year wolves are among the easiest to locate by their vocalizations. From late July through mid-October wolves are frequently heard from the Highway 60 vicinity. Wolves are social animals that travel in groups called packs. During midsummer, the pups are led from the dens to areas known as "rendezvous" sites, which are frequently beaver meadows (grassy areas where a beaver pond once existed) or bog edges. The pups are stationed at these sites and the adults bring them food from hunting excursions farther afield. Individual rendezvous sites may be used from several days up to several months at a time. While at these locations the pups are very vocal and readily respond to human howls.

It is important that we do not harass wolves or any animal, for that matter. If you are lucky and do have wolves respond to your efforts, enjoy their wild music and then move on. Getting them to repeatedly call back to you is unfair to the wolves and can be considered a form of harassment. It is also extremely important that you do not try to see them by walking in the direction they howled from. Wolves can be easily disturbed when they are at den or rendezvous sites, so please give them the respect they are due.

Try listening or howling (refer to **When and How to See Wildlife** in Chapter 3)) from the following locations:

- Western Uplands Backpacking Trail — KM 3. Try from the bridge across the Oxtongue River at the start of the trail.
- Arrowhon Road — 4.5 kilometres north from KM 15.4. Try at the intersection of this road and the old railway.
- KM 18. The bogs stretching to the south occasionally have wolves.
- Rock Lake Road — KM 40.3. Try at the intersection of the highway and Rock Lake Road; also try 2.8 kilometres south on Rock Lake Road.
- Sunday Creek — KM 42.6. The top of the rock cut just

west of Sunday Creek and on the north side of the highway is an outstanding site. The eastern edge of the rock has a gradual slope easily climbed, but be careful.

- Eos Lake — KM 43.8. Wolves are regularly heard north of the lake.
- Beaver Pond Trail — KM 45.2. Wolves have been heard on either side of the highway from the trail entrance.
- Opeongo Road - KM 46.3. Try at the junction of the highway and Opeongo Road; also try up the Opeongo Road at the culvert where Costello Creek crosses under the road approximately 3 km north of the highway.
- Brewer Lake — KM 48.6. I have only heard wolves here a few times, but the incredible echoes from across the lake make this an enjoyable spot to try.
- KM 54. Traditionally this has been a good spot. Wolves, when present, are usually heard north of the highway.

Although the above locations might offer a better chance of finding wolves, these animals have been heard at many other sites in the Corridor, including several highway campgrounds. However, I wouldn't recommend howling at these busy spots, particularly at 1:00 a.m!

Because you will be stopping along the highway, you must be safety conscious. Beware of soft shoulders on the roadside, but never stop on the pavement. If possible, pull off in parking lots of trails or picnic sites. Stand well off the highway when you are enjoying this magnificent music of the wilds.

Public Wolf Howls, excursions to hear wolves in the Corridor, are held on Thursdays in August if wolves have been located and weather permits. Since a Wolf Howl isn't attempted unless the naturalist staff has confirmed the presence of wolves the previous night, whether there will be a Howl is neither known nor disclosed until each Thursday morning. Thus, to determine if a Howl is being held on that day, either inquire at the Visitor Centre or any other Park office, or check the weekly bulletin This Week in Algonquin (the current issue is distributed each Thursday morning). If a Wolf Howl isn't held, an Evening Program will be offered instead.

Red Fox

People regularly encounter seemingly tame foxes in Algonquin. The tameness is invariably due to frequent contact with humans and not because of disease. Regardless, one should always be cautious and not touch or feed one of these animals. Although foxes are most active after sunset, they might be encountered in early morning or late evening. Probably the best way to find them is to drive the highway slowly after sunset and watch for their greenish eyes shining from the sides of the road.

One pair usually dens on the Airfield at Mew Lake (KM 30.6). Thus, they are often seen in the Lake of Two Rivers and Mew Lake section of Highway 60. Other good areas for seeing foxes are along the highway near Rock Lake Road (KM 40.3), the Visitor Centre (KM 43), and between the Algonquin Logging Museum (KM 54.6) and the East Gate (KM 56).

Black Bear

Although relatively common throughout the Park, black bears are usually quite difficult to see primarily because of their shyness. Fortunate visitors might view a bear in early morning or late evening, the optimal times for encountering one, either crossing the road or foraging along open edges.

Black bear sign is usually easier to find than the maker of it. When bears are feeding on berries, their droppings are often seen along road edges, especially logging roads, on the OA & PS railway bed (for its location, see the section under that name in this chapter), and in open areas along trails, especially Centennial Ridges. The seeds of the fruit and the colourful wash identify large swirled droppings as those of bear. While other animals, notably raccoon and large weasels, also feed on fruit, their droppings are smaller and more cylindrical. Other bear signs to watch for are claw marks and tangles of broken limbs in trees. In the late summer and fall, bears climb fruit-bearing trees. Cherry trees are the first to attract their attention. Later, bears focus on American beech and red oak. Tangles of broken limbs in the crowns of these trees and scarred-over claw imprints (particularly evident on beech trees) are the result of bear feeding episodes. The tangles, known as "bear nests," are sometimes viewed along some of the interpretive trails, including Mizzy Lake, which has a section of the trail devoted to bear sign. You can also see old bear claw marks on poplar trees, which bears climb in the spring to feed on new leaves. Such markings can be viewed on the Centennial Ridges trail, on your right between Post 1 and the split in the trail on top of the steep hill.

The best time of the year for seeing bears is mid-July to mid-August when raspberries, blueberries and cherries ripen. During this period, Opeongo and Rock Lake roads are worth driving slowly.

Very infrequently bears are encountered feeding on berry patches along trails. Generally they are long gone before you are even aware they were present. By walking trails as silently as possible (for if the bears hear you coming they quickly vanish), either as early or as late in the day as possible, you might increase your slight chances of seeing a bear.

One area to check during the berry season is the old mill site at Whitefish Lake, which is accessed by driving south on Rock Lake Road until you reach the left turn for Rock Lake Campground. Keep to the right and continue until you reach the bridge crossing the Madawaska River. *Do not obstruct the gate on the bridge.* You can walk across the bridge and follow the left fork of the road to the large open area where a sawmill once stood. The new grasses in spring and the berries in late summer make this a popular site for foraging bears.

Beavers get most active as the sun goes down.

Beaver

The most abundant of the larger mammals in Algonquin, beavers inhabit thousands of small ponds and lakes. The characteristic "V" wake of a beaver swimming across an Algonquin waterway is a common sight at sunset. Their dams adorn many a creek and small river on canoe routes all through the Park. Because much of beaver activity takes place at night, it is difficult to see them during the day. However, if you sit by a beaver pond in the evening, you should be rewarded by the appearance of one or more shortly after the sun disappears. As autumn passes, beavers get more and more active during daylight hours. By late October, most beavers are busy storing piles of branches in their ponds. Beavers do not hibernate but usually remain hidden from view inside their lodge or under the ice. The branch piles are their winter food supply. In the fall, beavers also add copious amounts of mud to the outside of their lodges. This insulation keeps the winter cold at bay. As October fades into November, both of these activities take place increasingly more often in daytime, making late autumn one of the best times to view these fascinating animals.

Beavers abandon and colonize sites regularly. You can generally tell if a pond is active by examining the dam and lodge. If freshly cut sticks adorn the dam or lodge, or if fresh mud has been applied to either structure, the odds are high that beavers are present.

The Beaver Pond Trail is an excellent trail not only for encountering beavers. The interpretive booklet gives a marvellous overview of the important ecology of this animal. The portion of the Mizzy Lake Trail that follows the OA & PS rail bed is another great place to view beavers. In addition, many of the lakes and ponds along Highway 60 also support colonies. Some of these allow you to watch beavers right from the comfort of your car, a particularly enjoyable venue during the biting fly season.

Some of the beavers along the highway sport silver "earrings." These are actually identification tags placed on the ears by researchers from the University of Guelph. Algonquin offers near-limitless wildlife and ecological research possibilities, and beavers have been popular subjects over the years.

Some of the traditional spots for viewing beavers, in addition to those already mentioned, are:

- Mew Lake - KM 30.1.
- Trailer Sanitation Station — KM 35.6. Check the pond approximately half a kilometre down the unpaved road beyond the gate at the north end of the parking lot.
- Eucalia Lake — KM 39. When visiting this excellent pond for beavers, one should park on the wider road shoulders below or above, not alongside, the guard posts bordering the pond.
- Ringneck Pond — KM 41.2. Check the pond on the south side as well as the north side of the road.

- Opeongo Road — KM 46.3. The best areas to check are the sections of creek immediately above and below the culvert where Costello Creek passes under the road (approximately 3 km north of the highway), and where Costello Creek flows into Opeongo Lake. This latter spot can be viewed either from the boat launches to the south of the Opeongo Store or from the road just before it enters the store and boat launch access area.
- South of Opeongo Road turn - KM 46.3. Walk in approximately 50 metres on the Bluff Lake Portage (across Highway 60 and slightly east of the Opeongo Road turnoff) to a beaver pond on your left.
- Brewer Lake — KM 48. Beavers are often seen in the evening from the parking lot overlooking the lake.

Otter

Otters can be challenging to find yet are frequently seen along the Corridor. They are more easily encountered either in late summer and fall when family groups are eating together, or in early spring when individuals are feeding along the edge of the receding ice. Otters range widely and it is difficult to predict where they will be from day to day. However, in early spring (mid-April to mid-May) they may frequent good feeding areas for several days or longer. They are often seen along the edge of the ice when the lakes begin to open. At this time of year it is useful to check any waterway for dark debris on the edge of the ice. These dark piles may be droppings or remains of meals, indicating the presence of otters.

In any season Costello Creek along Opeongo Road (KM 46.3) is one of the best spots to see them. They might be encountered virtually anywhere open water is visible and are occasionally observed on the logs in Costello Lake across from the picnic ground. The best area to check, however, is Costello Creek from the culvert where the creek flows under the road (approximately 3 km north of the highway) and where it enters Opeongo Lake. Other areas where you might find otters are:

- Mizzy Lake Trail — KM 15.4. Mizzy is without question the best trail for encountering otters. They might be seen in any of the nine ponds visible from the trail. In particular, Mizzy Lake and Wolf Howl Pond offer excellent opportunities to view these amazing animals.
- Little Madawaska — KM 21.4. The pond beside the pull-off on the north side of the highway occasionally has otters.
- Mew Lake — KM 30.1.
- Lake of Two Rivers Campground — KM 31.8. Otters are frequently present where the Madawaska River enters the lake.
- Ringneck Pond — KM 41.2.

Algonquin Birds

With its diverse array of habitats, particularly the mixture of northern coniferous and southern deciduous forests, Algonquin boasts an amazing mixture of species. Over half of the approximately 266 species recorded within the Park have been known to breed here. The majority of the nesting species can usually be encountered by searching the proper habitat, although frequently they are more easily heard than seen.

Two of the Park publications, *Birds of Algonquin Provincial Park* and the *Checklist and Seasonal Status of the Birds of Algonquin Provincial Park*, are invaluable in enjoying the birds found here. The first publication discusses birds by habitat and includes excellent colour photographs of 77 of the more common species. The latter summarizes all of the species recorded up to 1997 and provides useful bar graphs detailing their dates of occurrence.

Because of the popularity of Algonquin's birds, the interpretive program offers early morning interpretive Bird Walks and an Evening Program titled The Birds of Algonquin. Most of the interpretive trails traverse a number of habitats and thus offer a variety of birds. My favourite general trails for birdwatching are Whiskey Rapids and Beaver Pond trails. Spruce Bog Boardwalk and Mizzy Lake are two of the best trails for encountering northern species. Valuable tips on finding birds can be found in **OBSERVING WILDLIFE**.

Usually birders search for the northern "specialties" (birds whose ranges do not extend much farther south than Algonquin) during Park visits. With this in mind the better locations along the Corridor for some of these species will be provided. In addition, sites for encountering other popular species will be given.

Spruce Grouse

This tame northern grouse prefers the cool, dark recesses of northern bogs and boreal forest. For many birders Algonquin is the place of their first, and frequently only, sighting.

The males are at their ornate finest during the breeding season in April and early May. They strut around with their red eye combs inflamed and their tails noisily fanning. Males also perform "flutter flights" from the ground up to a nearby conifer and back down again. This noise often makes it easy to find a displaying bird. The males begin to show off again in early fall, but usually it is a more subdued performance. Tape recordings of female calls will attract the males, especially in spring. But before trying this read item number three in **Wildlife-viewing Etiquette** (in **OBSERVING WILDLIFE**).

Spruce Grouse are frequently observed in spruce and other conifers as they feed on the needles. Early morning and late afternoon are times of increased feeding activity in summer. From the middle of August to mid-September they feed on the needles of tamaracks. In late fall and winter the needles of spruces and pines are eaten. When searching for the birds, scan from ground level to about seven metres on the branches of coniferous trees. Listen for the snapping of needles while they are feeding. When flushed, Spruce Grouse exhibit a noisy, heavy flight that is usually very short in duration. An excellent article on finding this species was written by Ron Tozer and Ron

Pittaway and appears in *Ontario Birds*, volume 8, number 2, a copy of which is available upon request at the Visitor Centre.

There are several excellent places where one can search for the sometimes elusive Spruce Grouse, and they are listed according to general ease in finding the birds. Of course, in any of these sites the birds might be either surprisingly easy or impossibly difficult to locate.

Spruce Bog Boardwalk — KM 42.5

This has traditionally been one of the best spots along the highway for Spruce Grouse. While you might encounter the birds along any part of the trail, there are at least two sections where more frequent observations have been made. Between Post 1 and the open bog mat before Post 2 there is an island of drier, more open ground. You will see a number of footpaths where grouse seekers have wandered, particularly on the left (north) side. Another good section lies between posts 6 and 7.

Mizzy Lake Trail — KM 15.4

The best area for Spruce Grouse lies along the northern section of the trail in the Wolf Howl Pond vicinity, which can be reached by walking the trail (highly recommended for the diversity of birds that will be encountered), or by driving north on the Arrowhon Road to the old railway bed junction and turning right. When you reach a locked gate, be sure to park to one side so that you don't block the road. Then proceed eastward on foot approximately one kilometre to Wolf Howl Pond.

Spruce Grouse are frequently seen either right on the rail bed picking up grit or feeding in the conifers fringing the sides. The section of rail bed just west of Wolf Howl Pond is good, but the 100 metres or so of rail bed southeast of Post 6 often produce the best results.

Opeongo Road — KM 46.3

There are two excellent locations along this road for seeing Spruce Grouse. They are often seen picking up grit along the edge of the road, particularly at daybreak. However, foot searches just off the road may be required much of the time. The first place to look is the spruce woods bordering the left (west) side of the road 2.5 kilometres north from the highway. Grouse might be encountered from this point for about another half kilometre north, on either side of the road.

The second area worth checking is along the right (east) side of the road approximately half a kilometre north of the culvert where Costello Creek crosses under the road (about 3 km north of the highway). The birds usually reside in the strip of spruces between the road and the open bog mat to the east, but can be found on the other side of the road as well.

Mike's Bog — KM 54.2

To access this bog walk through the planted pines on the east side of the highway. An old road exists between the bog and the plantation. Travel down this road for about 200 metres and then walk down into the bog to your left.

Davies' Bog — KM 30

Another area to check if you still haven't succeeded is the coniferous forest surrounding Davies' Bog. This is usually a difficult spot to find them in, but they are here! The best way to access this site is to walk the Bat Lake Trail in reverse to Post 12. You might see Spruce Grouse on the trail, but odds are some searching will be required. Try scouring the spruces on either end of the boardwalk at Post 12.

Gray Jay

This northern bird is a delight to encounter, not only because of its gentle nature but also because it will readily take food from your hand. At times it seems hard

Gray Jays frequently find you before you find them.

to believe that a bird so seemingly meek could survive the severe Algonquin winters. Yet Gray Jays do so quite nicely, principally because they continually store food throughout the other seasons. It is fascinating to watch the birds in action. After accepting a morsel of bread, cookie, raisin or whatever your offering might be, the bird rolls each piece in its mouth, coating it with saliva. Then it flies off, stashing the package in a tree, frequently under a piece of lichen or loose bark. The saliva cements the package securely in the hiding place, which quite often is robbed by Blue Jays, experts in shadowing their cousins.

This sticky coating may also serve to keep the food fresh, for it may be many months before the stash is eaten.

When Gray Jays approach you for handouts, you will often find that their legs are decorated with colourful bands that jingle-jangle when they fly. Dan Strickland, longtime Chief Park Naturalist, has been studying these birds for more than 30 years. By banding the young each spring he has been able to document how long they live, as well as where they range and who they mate with.

This amazing study is one of the longest of its kind and is truly a labour of love for Dan. You can help by recording the dates and locations of your sightings of banded jays, plus the band colour combinations on each of their legs. For example, red over standard (a standard aluminum band that is always present on one of the legs) on the bird's left leg and yellow over dark green on the right leg. Your valuable observations can be dropped off at the Visitor Centre or at the gates, if that is more convenient.

Since Gray Jays frequent much the same habitat as Spruce Grouse, it comes as no surprise that you might well encounter both species in the same area. Thus, any of the aforementioned areas for seeing grouse might produce jays. Unfortunately there are times, particularly in late spring and early summer, when Gray Jays become secretive and tough to find, even in the best of locations. They become easier to find as summer progresses and are virtually guaranteed to be seen in fall and winter. Refer to **OBSERVING WILDLIFE** for tips detailing how you might attract them (although these birds tend to find you first!) and be sure to carry some spare food with you. Some regular "hot spots" to try are:

Opeongo Road — KM 46.3

Several pairs have territories along this road. While they might be encountered almost anywhere here, try at the Costello Picnic Grounds, at the junction of the logging road 2.5 kilometres north of the highway, and just past past the culvert where Costello Creek crosses under the road, 3 km north of the highway.

Mizzy Lake Trail — KM 15.4

The old railway at the northeastern section of the trail is the best area for them. They can usually be found between West Rose Lake and the gate near the junction of the rail bed and Arrowhon Road.

Spruce Bog Boardwalk — KM 42.5

The birds might find you virtually anywhere on this trail.

Mew Lake Campground — KM 30.6

Try walking around the northeast part of the campground, particularly in fall and winter.

Black-backed Woodpecker

Another "northerner" frequently sought by birders, Black-backed Woodpeckers also frequent the bog and coniferous habitats of the former two species. They are most easily encountered by listening for their slow, heavy pecking and their sharp calls, which sound like a noisy kiss to the back of your fingers. The best way, though, is to imitate or play back the call of a Barred Owl. Not only does this call draw in Black-backs, it is also guaranteed to attract any other woodpecker within hearing range. But before using playbacks read **Wildlife-viewing Etiquette** in **OBSERVING WILDLIFE**.

An aid to finding these birds involves the distinctive signs they leave behind when feeding. One of their favourite foods is the larvae of bark beetles, which tunnel, as their name suggests, under the bark of trees. Black-backed Woodpeckers particularly relish the species that inhabit spruces. To get at the beetles these woodpeckers strip the bark from large sections of infected trees. Thus, if you find spruces with large sections of the trunk recently stripped clean (the barkless trunk appearing orange), the woodpecker is probably not far away. These birds are year-round residents, and in summer they frequently nest near beaver ponds.

Sites where you might encounter these birds include all of the places described for Spruce Grouse, especially the northeastern section of the Mizzy Lake Trail and along Opeongo Road. I would also recommend you search at these other locations:

Western Uplands Backpacking Trail — KM 3

The section of the trail just past the bridge at the trail start is an excellent place for these birds.

Oxtongue Logging Road Pond — KM 8

This road, closed to private vehicles, leads north from the highway. Park either on the highway shoulder or to the side of the gate, leaving the access unobstructed. Walk approximately one kilometre along the road until you arrive at a large pond on the left. Black-backed Woodpeckers are often encountered near the pond.

Boreal Chickadee

This northern counterpart of the Black-capped Chickadee becomes extremely silent and thus next to impossible to find during the nesting season. However, as summer progresses they become increasingly vocal, and by mid-August they can be found in most of the locations frequented by Spruce Grouse and Black-backed Woodpecker.

In addition to the two locations listed for Black-backed Woodpeckers, both excellent for Boreal Chickadees in late summer, also try the following sites:

- The old railway bed on the north side of the highway — KM 22.3.
- The south edge of the Airfield past the Mew Lake Campground office — KM 30.6.
- The trail around the Algonquin Logging Museum KM 54.6

OTHER SPECIES

A few more of the commonly sought-after species will be profiled here. Additional information concerning any of the Park birds can be obtained from the naturalists at the Visitor Centre.

Barred Owl

The booming calls and eerie cackles of Barred Owls, Algonquin's most common owl, are regularly heard at night. They usually respond to playbacks of taped calls, such as those found on the inexpensive cassette *Voices of Algonquin*, and even answer to human imitations. Before using playbacks refer to **WILDLIFE-VIEWING ETIQUETTE** in Chapter 3. Barred Owls are also easily "squeaked in" (refer to **WHEN AND HOW TO SEE WILDLIFE** in the same chapter), particularly just before sunset.

You may wish to participate in an interpretive Night Walk if one is offered during your stay. Barred Owls are often encountered on these outings.

While you might hear these birds virtually anywhere in the Highway Corridor, some of the more regular locations are provided.

Western Uplands Backpacking Trail — KM 3

Try from the bridge at the beginning of the trail.

Whiskey Rapids Trail — KM 7.2

I have frequently heard Barred Owls from the highway near the trail entrance.

Hardwood Hill — KM 16.7

Barred Owls have traditionally been heard a few hundred metres along the logging road running north of the highway at this site, but can be occasionally heard on the south side of the highway as well.

Source Lake Road — KM 20.1

Approximately 0.4 kilometre north of the highway is a good place to try.

Hemlock Bluff Trail — KM 27.2

Barred Owls have been heard from both sides of the highway at this location.

Trailer Sanitation Station — KM 35.6

Try near the pond approximately half a kilometre north from the Sanitation Station turnaround.

Rock Lake Road — KM 40.3

Try at the intersection of this road and the highway. Also try one kilometre up the road on the north side of the highway at this intersection. Here you will encounter a gate marking the end to public travel on this road.

Spruce Bog Boardwalk — KM 42.5

I always enjoy listening from the top of the rock cut that lies between the parking lot and the bridge crossing the creek. The eastern edge of the rocks has a gradual slope, but take care in climbing up.

Brewer Lake — KM 48.6

The parking lot offers safe parking as well as an excellent listening location.

Leaf Lake Ski Trail — KM 53.9

I have heard Barred Owls in the vicinity of the trail entrance.

Pileated Woodpecker

This spectacular crow-sized woodpecker is common throughout Algonquin and is frequently encountered along Highway 60. Their easily recognized excavations, made in search of carpenter ants, can be seen in a number of dead trees along the highway edge. Usually they produce large, often gigantic rectangular or oval holes quite visible from a great distance. Listen for their distinctive *kuk-kuk-kuk*. An imitation of these or Barred Owl calls may attract the birds.

Pileated Woodpeckers frequently fly across the highway in late afternoon. Their stiff flight with massive wings flashing bold black-and-white patterns is quite distinctive.

These birds are common and can be found along any trail, particularly, but not exclusively, on trails through mature hardwood forests. Some locations where Pileated Woodpeckers are often seen include:

- Hardwood Lookout Trail — KM 13.8.
- Found Lake — KM 20. Right behind the Algonquin Gallery is a fine spot to search. A trail that encircles Found Lake starts directly behind the buildings.
- Highway 60 between KM 25.5 and KM 26.3.
- Highway 60 between KM 28.5 and KM 28.8.
- Rock Lake Road — south from KM 40.3.
- Booth's Rock Trail — nine kilometres south from KM 40.3.

Common Loon

This is a relatively easy bird to encounter because virtually all of the larger lakes support at least one pair. Even the busiest lakes usually have loons that produce young each year. It is an enjoyable sight to see a family group in action, with both parents feeding small fish to the one or two young, and also occasionally giving them rides on their backs. The vocalizations of this bird are an important part of many Algonquin experiences because its spine-tingling calls are among the wildest sounds in the world. Rare is the campsite near water that lacks their mournful wails and haunting laughter at night. The cassette *Voices of Algonquin* not only has outstanding recordings of these birds but also offers explanations as to what the different calls mean.

Because loons nest at the edge of the water, their nests are frequently discovered by canoeists. If you are

Lakes all through Algonquin usually have at least one pair of nesting loons in summer.

in a canoe and locate a nest, don't spend any more than a brief moment admiring the birds before you leave them in privacy. Repeated harassment, regardless of how unintentional it might be, may result in a loss of the eggs.

Loons are often seen in larger lakes right along the highway. Although generally distinctive birds, they might be confused with Common Mergansers, a fish-eating duck. Loons are larger with heavier heads and necks. In summer they display a bold checkered back pattern. The mergansers are smaller and females, which are the only adults present in summer, have reddish-brown heads that contrast with a gray back. Usually they have many more than two young in tow; in fact, the average brood size is 12. Viewing sites for loons include:

- Smoke Lake — KM 15.2.
- Lake of Two Rivers — KM 32.3 to KM 33; KM 33.8; KM 34.5.
- Costello Lake — KM 46.3.
- Brewer Lake — KM 48.6.

Scenic Views

The Highway Corridor is rich in striking scenery and breathtaking vantage points. Each season dresses the roadside scenery in new and dramatic apparel. Lakes come alive under the swirling mists of late summer, and in autumn the maple hills transform into an extravaganza of colour. **SEASONAL HIGHLIGHTS** details the best time for viewing fall colours.

Of course, beauty is in the eye of the beholder, and undoubtedly you will find a number of other sites along the highway that appeal to you. The following is simply a guide to some of the more dramatic locations for viewing and/or photography in the Highway Corridor.

Tea Lake — KM 9.2

The only drawback to this site are the telephone lines situated along the lake side of the highway.

Smoke Creek — KM 12

This creek offers excellent fall colours along its edge and also reflections of these in its water, particularly early in the morning.

Smoke Lake — KM 13.5

A good view of maple hills and Smoke Lake is offered at this point from the highway.

Hardwood Lookout Trail — KM 13.8

As its name suggests, this trail has a lookout over hardwood hills. The views from the other trails offering lookouts are generally more dynamic.

Smoke Lake — KM 14.8

The pull-off on the lake side is an ideal place to park. At daybreak in August the point jutting into Smoke Lake has the sun rising behind it. The mists that rise off the lake at this time of year create a backdrop that is simply outstanding.

Late summer morning mists add another element to the beauty of Smoke Lake and other Park waterways.

Hardwood Hill — KM 16.6

The view to the west is particularly striking during the peak of the fall colours.

Track and Tower Trail — KM 25

A superb view of Cache Lake is offered at Post 7.

Two Rivers Hill — KM 28.5

This view to the east is particularly attractive at daybreak. Mists frequently shroud the far hills, and the pine at the lower left of the hill projects nicely against this backdrop. A beautiful hardwood forest covers the hillside along the north side of the road and is quite attractive in the autumn.

Two Rivers Trail — KM 31

A fine lookout is afforded from Post 8.

Lake of Two Rivers — KM 32.5

Various points along the road offer excellent views of the lake. The far side of the lake is alive with colour in the fall. This spot is also spectacular at daybreak, particularly when cloaked with mists in late summer.

Centennial Ridges Trail — two kilometres south from KM 37.6

Some of the finest vantage points in the Corridor are situated along this rugged trail.

Lookout Trail — KM 39.7

An excellent view of the rolling hills typical of this side of the Park is available from the highway. Even after the maples have faded this site still offers colourful views when the hills blaze with golden poplars.

One of the most dramatic views of the western uplands is achieved from the top of this walking trail. An unmarked trail leading to a fine view is located directly across the highway from the west end of the parking lot. Remember that all lookouts lack railings, so make sure you keep children under control at all times.

Booth's Rock Trail — nine kilometres south of KM 40.3

The view over Rock Lake from Post 7 is simply spectacular.

Algonquin Visitor Centre — KM 43

The viewing deck at the Visitor Centre offers a breath-taking view, equally marvellous at any time of the year.

Costello Creek — 3.5 kilometres north from KM 46.3

This boggy creek with a dramatic cliff rising behind is a beautiful area year-round. Several spots along the road offer enjoyable views, especially in late summer and fall. My favourite view is from just beyond the culvert where Costello Creek passes under the road.

The OA & PS Railway was extremely busy in its heyday, with trains reportedly as frequent as every 20 minutes.

Brewer Lake — KM 48.6

The hillside across the lake contains some of the best fall colour along the highway. If you climb to the top of the rock cut on the north side of the highway, an even better view is offered.

HISTORICAL POINTS OF INTEREST

Algonquin has had a long and fascinating history. Evidence of activities in earlier times can often be located right along the Highway Corridor. The following is a brief guide to some of the more interesting historic sites located in the Corridor. Other sites in the highway vicinity but accessible only by canoe will be discussed under **Canoeing in the Corridor.**

The Ottawa, Arnprior and Parry Sound (OA & PS) Railway

The rail bed of this historic railway, reputed to have been one of the busiest in Canada with a train every 20 minutes, can be viewed at several locations. In fact, sections of the rail bed are utilized by three of the interpretive and both backpacking trails.

J.R. Booth, a lumber baron prominent in the Park's history, built this railway between 1894 and 1896. Initially it was used for hauling logs and grain, but soon it became important in transporting visitors to Algonquin. It remained the only way to reach the Park until the arrival of the highway in the mid-1930s.

The easy access provided by Highway 60 became the nemesis of the OA & PS. The section of railway between Lake of Two Rivers and Cache Lake was discontinued in 1933. Service from the east to Lake of Two Rivers was terminated in 1946, and from the west to Cache Lake in 1959.

For simplicity, access to the old railway bed will be given starting from the west end of the Park.

Mizzy Lake Trail — KM 15.4

The northeast section of the trail lies on the rail bed. This can also be reached by driving up Arrowhon Road approximately four kilometres to a crossroads. The road crossing Arrowhon Road is actually the rail bed of the OA & PS Railway.

Source Lake Road — KM 20

Drive north until you hit the dip at the Madawaska River (here just a small creek) crossing. The railway abutments are clearly visible on either side of the road.

Highway 60 Crossing — KM 22.3

You will see a small parking area on the north side of the road. The parking lot on the south side of the road is used by the staff of Camp Tanamakoon, a girls' camp. Although the railway actually crosses the highway, only the section on the north side is walkable. Look for a footpath leading northwest. As you face the woods, it will be to your left. After travelling through an alder thicket, you will enter an open area where the rail bed becomes apparent. If you continue, you will eventually reach Source Lake Road.

Cache Lake — KM 23.5

Drive into the Cache Lake parking lot. When you near the boat launch the rail bed can be easily viewed to your left behind the shelter. The section to your right is a little more difficult to see because a planation of pines obscures the rail bed. However, a footpath traverses the pines. This path is well worth exploring since it travels along the railway platform in front of the remnants of the Highland Inn, a grand railway hotel. The hotel was built in 1908 and expanded in 1910. This elegant building was demolished in 1957, two years before the rail service was discontinued from the west. All that remains are a few walls bordering the railway platform, moss-covered stairs leading up to the site of the inn and an old fire hydrant. If you travel east along the rail bed, you will arrive at the remains of a trestle that spanned a bay of Cache Lake.

Track and Tower Trail — KM 25

The railway bed forms part of this trail and the history of the railway is discussed in the trail guide booklet. The remains of several trestles can also be viewed from this excellent trail.

It is intriguing to think that during the First World War armed guards stood sentinel on these trestles to thwart potential saboteurs. Use of this section of the railway was discontinued in 1933.

Highland Backpacking Trail — KM 29.7

One can access the old railway bed by walking 2.8 kilometres on this trail. At this point the rail bed intersects the Highland Trail, and the section leading northeast forms part of the trail.

Airfield — KM 30.6

Drive past the campground office until you reach the parking lot on your left (the Airfield is straight ahead and you turn right to go to the Mew Lake Campground). The Old Railway Bike Trail crosses the Airfield to the Madawaska River where a bridge connects it to the old railway bed. You can also access the old rail bed by going to the extreme south-west corner of the Airfield and walking west on the road that brings you to the Track and Tower Trail. From Post 15, the trail follows the old rail bed.

Rock Lake — 7.5 kilometres south from KM 40.3

When you turn left at the end of the Rock Lake Road to access Rock Lake Campground and Booth's Rock Trail, you are now on the old railway bed. The rail bed is used as a road from this point to the parking lot for the Booth's Rock Trail. The last section of the Booth's Rock Trail also lies on this rail bed.

Other Historical Sites

A few additional points of interest are detailed here.

Tote Road and Building Remains — KM 7.2

These sites are located along the Whiskey Rapids Trail. The 45 kilometres of tote road extended from Dorset (west of Algonquin) to the north end of Canoe Lake and crossed the Oxtongue River at the Tea Lake Dam. Horse-drawn wagons in summer and sleighs in winter were used to haul supplies in the late 1800s. The tote road forms the portion of the trail between Post 10 and the parking lot. Between Posts 9 and 10 the rotting remains of either a halfway house or shelters used by river drivers are visible.

Tea Lake Dam — KM 8.1

The dam is located on the Oxtongue River at the end of the Tea Lake Dam Picnic Grounds. This modern dam, built in 1964, replaces a much earlier wooden version that Tom Thomson, one of Canada's most renowned artists, painted in 1915. It is believed that Thomson's first trip to Algonquin involved a camping trip to this very spot.

James Dickson Memorial — KM 20

Along the stairs to the Art Gallery you will find this memorial. Dickson was the provincial land surveyor who, through his recommendations and surveys, was instrumental in the formation of Algonquin Park. At the top of the stairs lies the Algonquin Gallery. This was formerly the Park Museum, which operated from 1953 to 1992.

Highland Inn — KM 23.5

This site is described in the Cache Lake entry in the **OA & PS Railway** section.

Airfield — KM 30.6

The Airfield, situated between Mew Lake and Lake of Two Rivers, can be reached by driving past the Mew Lake Campground office until you reach the parking lot on your left (the Airfield is straight ahead and you turn right to go the Mew Lake Campground).

This extensive open area was cleared in 1935 as an emergency landing strip for aircraft. Although never used for this purpose, planes have occasionally landed when short on fuel. It has also been used for a variety of activities, including fire control demonstrations and fly-in breakfasts. As well, conducted interpretive outings including Bird Walks are held here.

McRae Mill Site — KM 30.6

Only a few subtle remains identify the site of this former sawmill built in 1931 and last used in 1944. It lies along the old railway bed on the far side of the Madawaska River on the south edge of the Airfield. To access the site, follow the Old Railway Bike Trail across the Airfield and across the Madawaska River bridge until you reach the rail bed. Turn left on the rail bed (bike trail) and follow it until you reach the opening where the mill formerly stood.

Hammer and Sickle — KM 35.3

These figures with the year 34 can be discerned on the rock cut just to the east of the lane on the south side of the highway. It is wise to park past this point, possibly near the entrance to East Beach (KM 35.4), because cars unexpectedly speed over the hill from the Lake of Two Rivers direction. Since Highway 60 was built in the mid-1930s. It has been suggested that these figures were chiselled in the rock by a member of the Communist Party, which had some followers in Canada at that time.

McRae Mill Site — eight kilometres south from KM 40.3

The McRae Sawmill operated on this site from 1957 to 1979. To access the site, travel south on the Rock Lake Road until you reach the left turn that leads to the Rock Lake Campground and Booth's Rock Trail. Keep to the right until you reach the bridge and gate. Park off to the side to keep road access open and walk across the bridge. The mill site lies only a few hundred metres past the bridge. Either fork on the road will take you into the site.

Barclay Estate — nine kilometres south from KM 40.3

This site lies on the Booth's Rock Trail. You can take a shortcut to it by travelling backward on the trail along the old rail bed of the OA & PS Railway. When you turn right at Post 9, you will have reached the grounds of the estate.

The estate was built at the turn of the century by Judge George Barclay, who was a relative of J. R. Booth, the lumber baron who built the railway. The estate was last used in 1953, and all that remains now are foundations, tennis courts and the remnants of the docks.

Harkness Memorial — six kilometres north from KM 46.3

Dr. William John Knox Harkness, the man responsible for the establishment of the Harkness Laboratory of Fisheries Research, which is located at this site, is honoured here. The plaque is located on a cairn only a few hundred metres past the parking lot on the north side of the store. just walk along the road (closed to unauthorized vehicles) that hugs the shoreline past the parking lot. The cairn is situated on the point to the right of the first building you come to.

Dr. Harkness was a professor of limnology at the University of Toronto and was also chief of the Fish and Wildlife Branch of the Ontario Department of Lands and Forests.

St. Anthony Lumber Company Railway Spur Line — KM 52

Take the dirt road running east just south of West Smith Lake. Watch carefully for a trail on the north (left) side of the road, halfway between the highway and the end of this short road. The trail lies on the railway spur line that once ran from Whitney to Opeongo Lake. The line extended north from here to Little McCauley Lake and then south back to the highway at the north end of Brewer Lake. Short sections of both Highway 60 and Opeongo Road are now located along parts of the rail bed on which timber was once transported. The spur line was built in 1902 and was abandoned in 1926.

The site of a former sawmill is located along this spur line between West Smith and Whitney lakes. However, access may be difficult, since parts of this rail bed may not be passable due to erosion and dense tree growth.

Algonquin Logging Museum — KM 54.6

This museum exhibits a spectacular assortment of historical logging buildings, structures and equipment chronologically arranged along a scenic trail. While some of the buildings, such as the camboose (a log structure with bunks arranged around a large central fireplace), are accurate replicas, others, including two ranger cabins, are the original buildings transported from their former sites.

Other highlights include a steam locomotive and replicated log chute and dam. The William M., a steam-warping tug also known as an alligator, towed log booms across large lakes and is one of only three still in existence. This amazing steam-driven boat could travel both across water by use of paddle wheels and over land by winch and log skids. The entrance road crosses the St. Anthony Lumber Company Spur Line described in the entry of that title.

CANOEING IN THE CORRIDOR

My favourite way of exploring the Highway Corridor is by canoe. The pleasure of silently paddling along a winding river or creek and rounding a bend only to encounter a moose or heron is truly a wilderness experience. Regardless of how busy the season might be, if you paddle at daybreak your canoe will frequently be the only one out there. In addition to seeing more wildlife you get the added bonus of experiencing the most beautiful time of day.

Canoeing in the Corridor will also enable you to visit a number of historical sites as well as participate in special interpretive events. Be aware that each person in a canoe is required to have a regulation life jacket, now known by the fancy term Personal Flotation Device (PFD). In addition, some sort of bailing equipment, a spare paddle, a 50-foot piece of floating rope, and a PSD (Personal Signalling Device — i.e., a whistle) are currently required. A must for any canoe trip is the *Canoe Routes of Algonquin Provincial Park* map brochure, which is not only an essential navigational tool but also a wonderful keepsake of the trip.

Available Services

Canoes can be rented at the Portage Store (KM 14.1), the Opeongo Store (north from KM 46.3) and Bartlett

Lodge (on Cache Lake south from KM 23.5). The first two rental places also offer canoe pickup and delivery, as well as complete outfitting services.

Free canoe demonstrations and lessons are usually offered in summer at various campground beaches. Check *This Week in Algonquin* and the bulletin boards to see if these are being offered during your visit.

The Portage Store in some years offers guided day outings for which the fee includes all equipment and a lunch. The Park Interpretive Program offers free guided outings where participants bring their own equipment (frequently rented from one of the stores) and a lunch.

These casual outings offer some canoeing instruction but focus on the Park's natural and human history encountered on the outing.

Canoe Centres on Canoe and Opeongo lakes sell permits and provide free information and advice for Interior canoeing and camping. *The Canoe Routes of Algonquin Provincial Park* map brochures are available here as well as at the gates and museums.

Recommended Short Trips

The Highway Corridor is a doorway into the Park Interior. Here there are a number of different access points from which to start overnight trips. In this section only excursions of a day or less will be discussed. For a description of highlights requiring longer trips refer to **THE PARK INTERIOR** in Chapter 8.

The following trips are all quite short, often a half day at most, but several have the option of being extended into a full day (or even longer) excursion if desired. It is always a good idea to pack some food and beverages even for a half-day trip. Remember that cans and bottles are prohibited from the Park Interior and that Interior camping permits must be obtained if you decide to stay overnight.

The Oxtongue River — (KM 3)

This is a beautiful river to canoe because it gently twists

and bends through its length. The spruces and firs that line its shores frequently harbour northern birds such as Boreal Chickadees and Black-backed Woodpeckers. The "quick-three-beer" whistles of Olive-sided Flycatchers follow you around each bend, and the incessant chatter of red squirrels continually scolds your intrusion. Great Blue Herons frequently flush ahead, while Common Mergansers spatter across the river's surface.

There are many options for accessing this river, including starting at the Portage Store on Canoe Lake and paddling down through Bonita into Tea Lake. Once on the river, only a couple of short portages (trails identified by black-and-yellow signs depicting a canoe being carried, used for bypassing rapids) are encountered between the Western Uplands Backpacking Trail and the starting point.

Another option, one which I frequently use, is to launch at the Western Uplands Backpacking Trail and paddle west to the first portage at Lower Twin Falls. About halfway down this route there is one short stretch of shallow water (shown as rapids on the *Canoe Routes of Algonquin Provincial Park* map brochure) where you may wish to walk your canoe through. To be sure, it is always best to wear running shoes when canoeing! You can also carry your canoe around the south side. When the water is high, you can float over the rocks, but my experience is that this usually isn't the case.

Watch for the beautiful trumpet-shaped nets of caddisflies, which lie on the upstream side of these gentle rapids. The current enters the net's large opening and passes through to the narrow end where the insect larva waits for the minute particles of food to arrive.

The portage around Lower Twin Falls is an excellent place to end this part of the trip. The rocks along the pretty little falls, actually more of a rapids, offer excellent sites on which to have lunch.

If you feel like continuing down the river, another short portage lies less than a half kilometre ahead. This is a tricky one, since the banks are steep and the current strong. If you are planning to continue, beware of this awkward portage and be prepared in advance to hug the south (left) shoreline as you approach the rapids.

If you are travelling with another couple and have the luxury of a second vehicle, you may wish to leave one just past the Park boundary where a short portage will bring you to the highway from the river. This allows you to paddle downstream the entire trip. Be aware of the extra distance involved and that the second portage west of the Western Uplands Backpacking Trail is only about halfway to the Park boundary.

The Madawaska River — (KM 35.4)

This trip is one of my favourite routes, not just because of this delightful winding river but also due to the plentiful wildlife I have encountered along its length. The route also holds a special place in my heart since I spend time at its source (Source Lake) in the summer and live at its mouth (Arnprior, where it joins the Ottawa River) in the winter. I generally put in my canoe at the boat launch at the Lake of Two Rivers East Beach (KM 35.4). From here I journey down to Whitefish Lake and back. Of course, one can make this a longer trip if desired, for it is an easy journey to Rock Lake from Whitefish. If you are camping at Pog Lake Campground, you can start paddling from the lake, since the Madawaska flows through it. There is only one very short portage around Pog Lake Dam.

I have often met moose, otter, Great Blue Herons, Common Mergansers, muskrats and American Black Ducks on this river. There are some excellent stretches that are bordered by northern woods where Boreal Chickadees and Gray Jays might be found. Another attraction is the historic OA & PS Railway, which follows the river for much of this route. Watch for the old culverts, in particular the one constructed of stones, which you pass by on the right (west) side of the river between Lake of Two Rivers and Pog Lake Dam. The more modern circular one contains a beaver dam.

Also watch in the water for the incredible green growth of freshwater sponge that covers submerged rocks and logs, particularly just below the dam. Sometimes it looks like fingerlike extensions; other times it appears as circular patches on the rocks. Be sure to pick up a piece (carefully so as not to upset the canoe) to feel its peculiar texture and sniff the curious aroma. If you are paddling along this route in late summer, keep your eyes peeled for the bizarre white blooms of turtlehead, an uncommon flower in Algonquin that peeks from the shores below the dam.

At the point where the Madawaska River meets the bay at the north end of Whitefish Lake (where the group campground is situated) you will come across a shallow area on the left side of the creek. When you get there, look carefully for snapping turtles that lie submerged with only their snouts projecting out of the water.

Once you reach Whitefish Lake, the large sand beach at the group campground is a perfect spot to have lunch and a swim. Alternately you can paddle over to the rocky points directly across the bay or along the east shore. From there you can either continue down Whitefish Lake or return. The top end of Whitefish Lake is really a river, but it eventually widens before reaching Rock Lake. If you are travelling with another couple, you might consider leaving a vehicle at Rock Lake and make this a one-way trip. Be aware, however, that motorboats are permitted on Whitefish and Rock lakes.

Costello Creek — north from KM 46.3

Even though this trip is shorter than the two previously discussed routes and follows a public road for a short part of its length, Costello Creek remains one of my favourite Algonquin waterways. Not only have I encountered numerous animals on this creek, but the scenery is frequently so stunning that I just stop paddling and become absorbed in the surrounding beauty. Several of the photographs in Algonquin Seasons were taken along this creek.

Costello Creek is one of my favourite waterways for a morning outing.

The best access is from the boat launch by the Opeongo Store. Just past the store there are parking lots where you can leave your vehicle. Motorboats are allowed on Opeongo Lake but cannot travel on Costello Creek. A sign indicating that motorboats are prohibited is situated on the tiny island just south of the boat launch.

Try starting your trip at the crack of dawn. At this time there is usually little wind, and wildlife is far more active, unlike humans. Canoe south from the docks into the narrowing of Opeongo that becomes Costello Creek. On the left side is an open floating bog where the carnivorous bog plants sundew and pitcher plant can easily be found. A number of beaver lodges, some active, are also located along the edge of this bog mat.

When you enter the narrow channel before the creek opens up again, beware of a couple of large submerged rocks that might scrape the bottom of your canoe. There is a deep channel here, so only a little bit of care is required to avoid these infrequent objects.

After the narrows, the creek winds through a fairly extensive bog mat punctuated with cattail clumps near this end. Great Blue Herons frequently fly just ahead of your canoe and land a couple of bends farther along, only to be flushed when you again draw near. Sometimes you will paddle around a bend and meet up with an American Bittern. Although they will fly to escape, occasionally they point their beaks into the air and freeze, relying on their breast stripes to blend in with the vegetation and render them invisible. Their strange song, resembling a stake being driven into soft mud, is often heard along the creek. Dead trees resulting from raised water levels in the lake provide homes and perches for a variety of birds. Tree Swallows twitter and Eastern Kingbirds angrily buzz over your canoe as you approach them. The "quick-three-beer" whistles of Olive-sided Flycatchers taunt you from the tops of these snags, while the sleepy "sweet-sweet-Canada-Canada-Canada" of White-throated Sparrows drift from the spruces.

As soon as you pass through the narrows, the overwhelming beauty of this route becomes apparent. The open expanse of bog mat is bordered by a neat fringe of black spruce and tamarack. These trees start out large near the high ground but shrink in size as they approach the open creek. Farther along, a rugged cliff towers to the east of the creek. This dramatic scenery is transformed into a wonderland in August when glowing mists swirl into the warming rays of the rising sun.

Moose feed in the creek in early summer, and I have also observed deer frequenting its edges. Otters inhabit the creek and mink hunt along it. Watch for droppings of these animals in the crevice of the huge boulder that you eventually paddle around. Just past this boulder is a small "island" on the right that is a wonderful spot for a rest or a lunch break. Just beyond that lies Opeongo Road. If you wish to continue along the creek, you can carry the canoe over the road or, if the water is high, you can paddle under it through the culvert.

If you walk along the paved road on the south side of

the culvert, on your left you will encounter a footpath leading up the hillside. There are large scattered rocks along the hill that will offer you a view over part of the creek you have just canoed. They also make good seats for lunch.

Other Day Trips

While the aforementioned are my favourite three routes, a number of other trips are available. These, however, include lakes on which motorboats are allowed (none of the above routes have motorboat activity, apart from the very end of the Madawaska route in Whitefish Lake and the start of the Costello Creek route at Opeongo Lake). Also, with their larger expanses of water these lakes can be a challenge to paddle on a windy day. However, a number of fascinating historical sites are situated along some of these routes, so if the day is calm, you may wish to try them.

Canoe Lake — KM 14.1

Canoe Lake is one of the busiest lakes in the Park, largely because it is the major launching point for canoe trips into the Interior. Motorboats also ply its waters, taking leaseholders to their cottages or carrying people and supplies to the children's camps (Wapomeo and Ahmek) situated on the lake. I would recommend canoeing on this lake as early as possible in the morning when motorboat activity might be low. However, you will undoubtedly meet a few on the return trip.

The north end of the lake is where everything of interest is located. On the north-central point lies a cairn well worth visiting. A small dock offers a place to access the short footpaths leading to the cairn. A rather obtrusive totem pole erected beside the cairn by a neighbouring camp is an obvious sign that you are at the right spot. The cairn was erected in September 1917 in honour of the famous Canadian artist Tom Thomson, who drowned in Canoe Lake on July 8, 1917. Friends of Thomson, including artists who later became known as the Group of Seven, erected this monument. The wording on the bronze plate was composed by J.E.H. MacDonald. The epitaph on the plaque is so moving that I feel compelled to reprint it here in case you don't get the opportunity to visit the cairn:

To the memory of Tom Thomson, artist, woodsman and guide, who was drowned in Canoe Lake, July 8, 1917. He lived humbly but passionately with the wild. It made him brother to all untamed things of nature. It drew him apart and revealed itself to him wonderfully. It sent him out from the woods only to show these revelations through his art, and it took him to itself at last.

As the inscription states, Thomson drowned in this very lake. His death is shrouded in controversy that has fuelled much conjecture and even a book and movie. Whether he drowned accidentally or was killed is of no consequence to this publication. Let it be enough that the magnificence of Algonquin captured his heart and that this beauty lives on through his art.

On the far shore directly west of the cairn lies the former townsite of Mowat. Established by the Gilmour Lumber Company in 1893, Mowat was also the site of the first Park headquarters. By 1896 at least 600 men lived here. However, the thriving lumber town soon became quiet when the mill closed down in 1900, following the bankruptcy of the Gilmour Company. Apparently the bankruptcy was at least in part due to a failed and incredibly costly scheme to transport logs from Mowat to Trenton. The logs were floated down Canoe Lake and the Oxtongue River to Lake of Bays. An alligator dragged the booms to Baysville where an endless chain-and-trough system dragged the logs overland to Raven Lake. From here logs were eventually floated down the Trent River system. Unfortunately the journey took so long that by the time the logs arrived at their destination they were in such poor shape that they were practically unusable.

Mowat soon became popular with tourists. A lodge

was opened in 1913 and became the summer headquarters for Tom Thomson. The busy atmosphere at Mowat was short-lived, however. Mowat Lodge burnt down in 1920, was rebuilt at a new location, then burnt down again in 1930. The once-thriving town of Mowat finally deteriorated into a virtual ghost town.

North from the Mowat townsite the rail bed of the OA & PS Railway is accessible by taking either of the two branches of the lake. The left branch travels up picturesque Potter Creek to the railway bridge. The right branch will eventually bring you to the old rail bed along the bottom of Joe Lake, but first you have to make a short portage around Joe Lake Dam. Two major buildings were situated in this area. Joe Lake Station was located along the rail bed near the bridge just above the dam, while the Algonquin Hotel, built in 1908, was situated on the hill between the dam and the rail bed on the west side of the waterway.

Smoke Lake — KM 14.1

Nominigan Lodge formerly lay on the point on the north side of the large bay approximately one-third of the way down the east side of the lake. As an extra point of reference, the site is due north of Molly Island. The lodge was built in 1913 and accommodated guests who arrived at Algonquin Park Station on Cache Lake. A horse-drawn taxi would deliver visitors from the train station to the lodge for a dollar per person. The lodge was dismantled in 1977.

The main historic attraction is the remnants of a log chute on the creek on the east side of the portage between Smoke and Ragged lakes. This wooden chute, typical of those built throughout Algonquin from the mid-1800s to the early 1900s, was vital in transporting logs over damaging rapids and waterfalls. All that remains of this chute, built in 1896, is a scattering of rotten timbers and planks.

Rock Lake — eight kilometres south from KM 40.3

Access to the lake can be achieved from the boat launch at the bottom end of the Rock Lake Road or from the beach beside the Booth's Rock Trail parking lot.

Of particular interest are some archaeological sites on the west side of the lake across from the campground. As you paddle along the west shore, heading south from where the Madawaska River enters the lake, you will come to a series of cottages. just before the first cottage you will see an opening with foundations of a former building. Land here. If you walk north from the west edge of the clearing and parallel to the shoreline, you will soon enter a group of hemlocks (there may be orange flagging tape marking the route). Among the trees are a number of shallow pits, difficult to find because they are obscured by years of debris falling into them. These are known as "vision pits." The natives would lie in these small depressions, possibly for days on end, until they experienced a vision. Please do not disturb the site in any fashion.

While the pits may not be impressive to see, the rock piles that were erected in memory of the visions certainly are. To locate these climb the steep hillside in a south-westerly direction on about a 45-degree angle from the pits. Orange flagging tape may indicate the route to this site. After you have climbed for several minutes, you should reach a plateau below a second rise. Along this plateau are situated the moss-covered rock piles erected by the Indians.

The rail bed of the OA & PS Railway follows the eastern shoreline from the campground down to the large point about halfway along the east side of the lake. The remains of the Barclay Estate buildings, described earlier in Other Historical Sites, are found on this point, and the remnants of the large docks are visible on its south side.

On the west shore directly across from the point lies another archaeological site. Indian pictographs were once visible on the cliff faces, but over time they have almost faded.

Sunday Creek — KM 42.7

Unlike the former routes, this one follows a winding creek to a couple of small lakes south of Highway 60. You can put in right from the highway, but it may be wise to park across the road in the Spruce Bog Board-walk parking.

Sunday Creek is a pretty, meandering creek that takes you to Norway and Fork lakes. At least two beaver dams block the creek, so be prepared to step out of the canoe and pull over them. Besides a close look at a bog and boreal forest along part of the route, you will also see the Visitor Centre on the ridge to the east of the creek.

Norway and Fork lakes are beautiful locations where you might come across moose. If you are here in late summer, be sure to try wolf howling along this route. Wolves travel through this area and will often answer back.

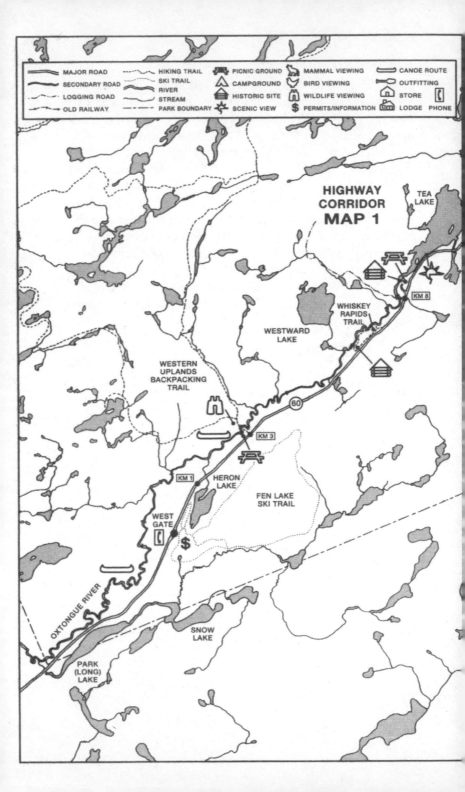

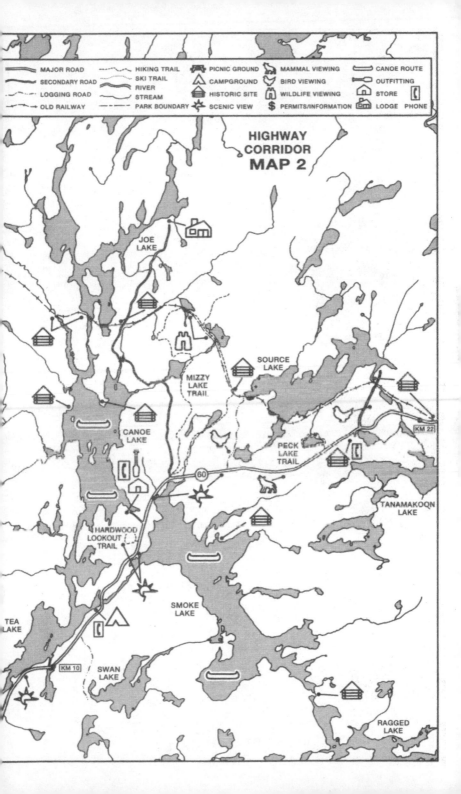

Legend

MAJOR ROAD	HIKING TRAIL	PICNIC GROUND	MAMMAL VIEWING	CANOE ROUTE
SECONDARY ROAD	SKI TRAIL	CAMPGROUND	BIRD VIEWING	OUTFITTING
LOGGING ROAD	RIVER	HISTORIC SITE	WILDLIFE VIEWING	STORE
OLD RAILWAY	STREAM	SCENIC VIEW	PERMITS/INFORMATION	LODGE PHONE
	PARK BOUNDARY			

HIGHWAY CORRIDOR MAP 2

JOE LAKE

SOURCE LAKE

MIZZY LAKE TRAIL

KM 22

CANOE LAKE

PECK LAKE TRAIL

60

TANAMAKOON LAKE

HARDWOOD LOOKOUT TRAIL

SMOKE LAKE

TEA LAKE

KM 10

SWAN LAKE

RAGGED LAKE

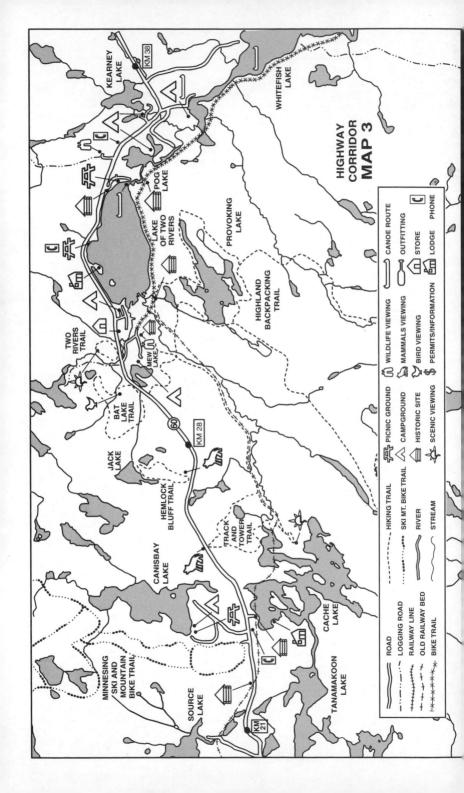

HIGHWAY CORRIDOR
MAP 3

Legend:

WILDLIFE VIEWING
MAMMALS VIEWING
BIRD VIEWING
PERMITS/INFORMATION
PICNIC GROUND
CAMPGROUND
HISTORIC SITE
SCENIC VIEWING
CANOE ROUTE
OUTFITTING
STORE
LODGE
PHONE

ROAD
LOGGING ROAD
RAILWAY LINE
OLD RAILWAY BED
BIKE TRAIL
HIKING TRAIL
SKI MT. BIKE TRAIL
RIVER
STREAM

KEARNEY LAKE
KM 38
WHITEFISH LAKE
POG LAKE
LAKE OF TWO RIVERS
PROVOKING LAKE
HIGHLAND BACKPACKING TRAIL
TWO RIVERS TRAIL
MEW LAKE
BAT LAKE TRAIL
KM 28
JACK LAKE
HEMLOCK BLUFF TRAIL
CANISBAY LAKE
TRACK AND TOWER TRAIL
MINNESING SKI AND MOUNTAIN BIKE TRAIL
SOURCE LAKE
KM 21
CACHE LAKE
TANAMAKOON LAKE

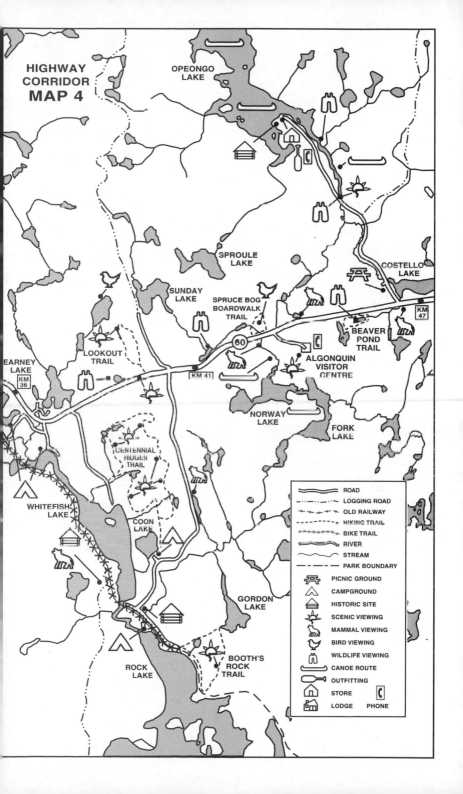

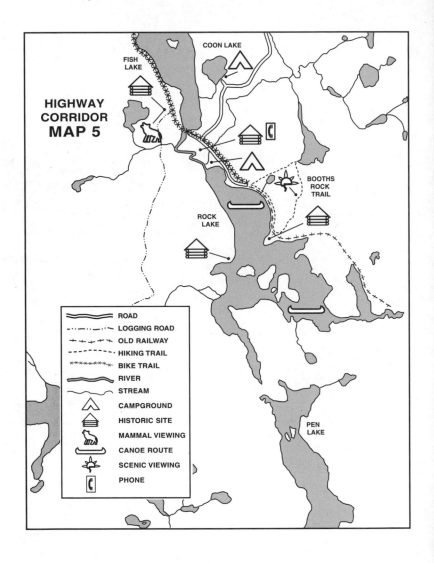

FISH LAKE

COON LAKE

HIGHWAY CORRIDOR MAP 5

BOOTHS ROCK TRAIL

ROCK LAKE

PEN LAKE

ROAD
LOGGING ROAD
OLD RAILWAY
HIKING TRAIL
BIKE TRAIL
RIVER
STREAM
CAMPGROUND
HISTORIC SITE
MAMMAL VIEWING
CANOE ROUTE
SCENIC VIEWING
PHONE

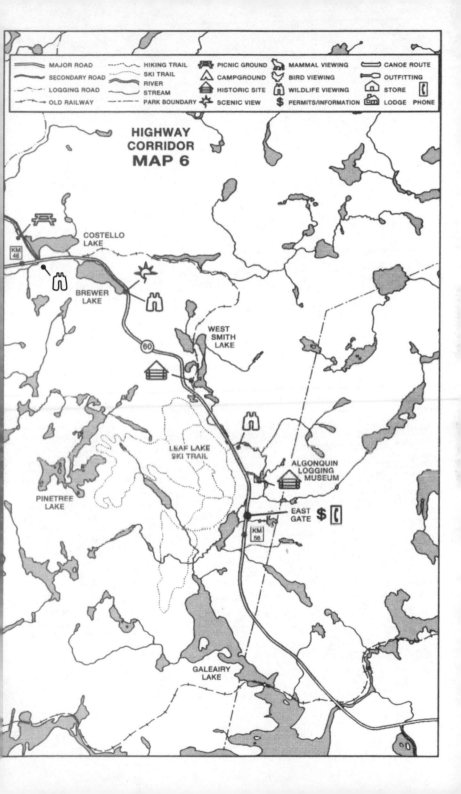

Legend

MAJOR ROAD	HIKING TRAIL	PICNIC GROUND	MAMMAL VIEWING	CANOE ROUTE	
SECONDARY ROAD	SKI TRAIL	CAMPGROUND	BIRD VIEWING	OUTFITTING	
LOGGING ROAD	RIVER	HISTORIC SITE	WILDLIFE VIEWING	STORE	
OLD RAILWAY	STREAM			LODGE	PHONE
	PARK BOUNDARY	SCENIC VIEW	PERMITS/INFORMATION		

HIGHWAY CORRIDOR MAP 6

KM 46

COSTELLO LAKE

BREWER LAKE

60

WEST SMITH LAKE

LEAF LAKE SKI TRAIL

PINETREE LAKE

ALGONQUIN LOGGING MUSEUM

EAST GATE $

KM 56

GALEAIRY LAKE

Although busier in recent years, the East Side of Algonquin sees dramatically fewer visitors than the Highway 60 Corridor. Yet the East Side offers many of the same services available along Highway 60, including a public campground, interpretive trails and a number of access points to the Interior. The rugged landscape and coniferous forests give this side of the Park a distinctive beauty and "feel" quite different than that of the western uplands.

Pine and poplar forests dominate the landscape, and a number of the plants and animals they support are either more common here or are not found on the West Side of the Park. Cardinal-flower and poison ivy, both virtually

Algonquin's eastern reaches exhibit forests of poplar and pine.

unknown along the Highway Corridor, occur with some frequency here. This part of Algonquin offers excellent wildlife-viewing opportunities and many species, including white-tailed deer, moose, black bear and wolf, are frequently encountered. Whether you are here for one day or several, many historical as well as natural history sites can be reached with reasonable ease.

Access is achieved from Highway 17 just west of Pembroke at the first Petawawa exit. Turn south on Renfrew County Road 26 (opposite the airport sign). After travelling only 0.3 kilometre, turn right on Renfrew County Road 28 (Barron Canyon Road). This road is paved for the next nine kilometres. Starting from the point where the pavement ends, every kilometre is marked with a black-and-white sign. These markings continue to the end of public access at Lake Travers (72 kilometres farther along). Points of interest will be referenced in the same fashion as was done for the Highway Corridor. For example, the Sand Lake Gate lies just before the 18-kilometre marker, and its location will be given as KM 18. Be aware that this gravel road is full of twists and turns, so do drive slowly.

There is a short access road leading to Mallard and See lakes at KM 15.2. You must obtain permits if you wish to visit these lakes. As is the rule for all of Algonquin, travellers must purchase and display permits for either day, campground, or Interior use. These can be purchased at the Sand Lake Gate and are necessary for visits to these lakes.

From the gate the road extends another 54 kilometres to Lake Travers. There are two public access roads branching from BNarron Canyon Road, one at KM 24 (leading to McManus Lake) and another at KM 37.8 (leading to Achray on Grand Lake). You will also encounter a number of logging roads running off both sides of the main road; they are closed to public vehicular travel and are posted to that effect.

The roads inside this part of Algonquin are unpaved and during dry periods they become quite dusty. Unless you enjoy a genuine "sandwich," you should prepare to roll up your windows when a cloud of dust from an approaching car draws near.

The East Side lacks gasoline and food services. Thus, you should make sure your vehicle is gassed up and that all of your food requirements are satisfied before you arrive. The Algonquin Portage Store is located 21 kilometres east of the Sand Lake Gate and offers meals, groceries, complete outfitting, bed and breakfast, and gasoline.

INTERPRETIVE WALKING TRAILS

As along Highway 60, trail guides are available in dispensers at the beginning of the interpretive walking trails. They can also be purchased in advance from The Friends of Algonquin Park (address in the appendix **IMPORTANT SERVICES**).

Barron Canyon Trail — KM 28.9

The East Side boasts one of the most spectacular and unique trails in all of Algonquin, possibly eastern Canada. The Barron Canyon Trail visits, as its name suggests, a magnificent gorge along the Barron River. The trail, only 1.5 kilometres long, leads to the top of the canyon, 100 metres above the river.

This spot has always been one of my favourites in Algonquin. The rugged lichen-encrusted rocks of the canyon are part of the ancient Canadian Shield. Continual erosion and expansion of the canyon, largely caused by the actions of frost, is evidenced by the rock rubble known as talus slopes lying at the cliff bases. Far below the clifftop the Barron River appears as a tranquil ribbon of water. In earlier times, however, it was a raging glacial river flowing with the power of a thousand Niagaras. Long after the glaciers retreated farther north the icy water draining through here still maintained a cold environment in the canyon. Evidence of this is found not only in the types of plants growing on the cliff faces but also in the species of animals in the water

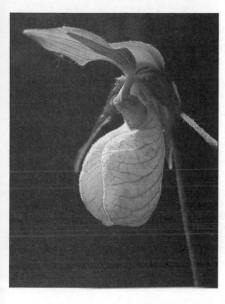

*Pink lady's-slippers
are common in East
Side pine forests by
early June.*

below. Several types of northern plants, four kinds of cold-water crustaceans and one species of Arctic fish reside within the confines of the canyon, all relics of earlier populations.

A strange mixture of birds also makes its home here. Yellow-bellied Flycatchers, a boreal species, are common, as well as wetland-loving Common Yellow-throats. Red-tailed Hawks join Common Ravens and Turkey Vultures in soaring on thermals rising from the gorge. The soft trills of Dark-eyed Juncos join the abrupt inflections of Eastern Phoebes echoing throughout the canyon.

Besides supporting an interesting mixture of life, Barron Canyon offers breathtaking views. Because the trail visits the edge of a cliff make sure children and pets are under physical control when you are walking here.

Berm Lake Trail — five kilometres south from KM 37.8

The Berm Lake Trail begins at the end of the large parking area to your left as you approach the stone building at Achray.

This beautiful trail takes you around Berm Lake through a typical East Side pine forest. The ecology of this forest type is discussed in the trail guide.

With the fragrance of pines filling the air and carpets of lichens and mosses cushioning the rocks, the trail is a delight to walk. In early June pouches of pink lady's-slippers adorn the trail, adding yet another element of form and colour to the landscape.

This trail is part of the Achray Trail System, and you can extend your walk by connecting with the Eastern Pines Backpacking Trail. Be sure you have a *Backpacking Trails of Algonquin Provincial Park* map (available at the Achray office and Sand Lake Gate) if you choose to use this longer trail. There are some spectacular sites on the backpacking trail, including a dramatic glacier-boulder garden and a magnificent set of waterfalls.

BACPACKING TRAILS

The Eastern Pines Trail is a fantastic trail offering a total distance of between 16.7 to 17.2 kilometres, depending on which loops you take. While there are a number of Interior campsites (which can be and perhaps should be reserved), the entire trail can be walked in a single day. There is but one large hill to climb and much of the trail follows relatively level ground so as long as you allow yourself plenty of time for breathers, this is quite feasible. Do bring water and food, though, for the all-day trek.

The trail skirts several lakes, including Johnston on which Great Blue Herons and Ospreys currently nest. One loop of the trail visits a collection of gigantic boulders left behind by the glaciers about 10,000 years ago. Another loop brings you to the stunning High Falls. The views of the cascading water make this alone worth the trip. Many people take advantage of the natural water slide for a cooling swim. The falls can also be accessed by canoe, either from the Barron River (accessed at Squirrel Rapids or Brigham Lake), or via Stratton Lake (accessed from Grand Lake at Achray).

The Backpacking Trails of Algonquin Provincial Park map can be purchased at the Sand Lake Gate or the Achray office.

HORSE TRAILS

Currently, there are two horse trails on the East Side. The Lone Creek Trail is a 30 kilometre trail that starts halfway down the McManus Lake Road (north from KM 24). A few Interior campsites are located near the parking area. The White Partridge Lake Horse Trail is a 16 kilometre trail that starts at Stuart's Spur, just south of KM 67, and leads to White Partridge Lake, where there is a camping area. Day Use and Interior Camping permits can be obtained at the Sand Lake Gate. For more information and updates on the trails call the Algonquin Park Information Office (705-633-5572) or the Operations North Office (613-732-5551).

FACILITIES AND INTERPRETIVE PROGRAM

Unlike the Highway Corridor, the East Side doesn't offer restaurants, lodges, or outfitting services. However, an interpretive program is currently conducted for several days each week (centred on weekends) in summer. Evening programs are held in the building on the north side of the main parking area and Algonquin for Kids programs and interpretive walks are conducted on nearby trails. The events are listed in the weekly flyer *This Week in Algonquin, Achray Campgound*, which is posted on the Sand Lake Gate and Achray Campground information boards, and is available as a handout at the Gate and the Achray Office.

At the time of writing, plans are being developed to use the Out-Side-In Cabin beside the Achray Office as an interpretive facility.

The Algonquin Portage Store, 21 kilometres outside the gate, offers outfitting and canoe shuttle services into this part of Algonquin, as well as gasoline.

Picnic Grounds

The only formal picnic ground is situated on the Barron River at Squirrel Rapids (KM 20.3). There is also a parking lot for canoe trippers who launch from this site. Excellent places can be found at Achray to have lunch. Tables and barbecue stands are situated to the west of the stone building and boat launch. In addition, the drive-in camping site at Pretty Lake (KM 54.5) is a fine place to eat.

Campgrounds

The one campground on the entire East Side is situated at Achray, on Grand Lake. This is accessed by driving five kilometres south from KM 37.8. Of all the camp-grounds in Algonquin this is one of the best-situated in terms of aesthetics. Grand Lake, as its name suggests, is one of the most exquisite lakes in all of Algonquin. Dramatic hills line the far side of the lake while extensive sand beaches border the campground shoreline. it is intriguing to think that Tom Thomson, who stayed in the log cabin between the stone office and the east pocket of the campground, admired and sketched the same sensational scenery that currently captivates us.

The campground lacks showers and laundry facilities but does have flush toilets. However, the superb beaches and splendid scenery more than make up for the absence of certain "conveniences."

At the time of writing, there is a single Yurt (Furnished Tent — see **CAMPGROUNDS** in Chapter 5) on a beautiful sand beach to the west of the Achray Campground. This can be accessed by foot (an old road travels from the campground to it) or by canoe. It is situated beside the rocky hillside from which Tom Thomson sketched his famous "The Jack Pine." Reservations (1-888-ONT-PARK) must be used if you wish to rent the yurt, which is not available in the winter months.

Apart from canoeing to Interior campsites, one alternative exists to the campground at Achray. There is an Interior site on Pretty Lake (KM 54.5) that can be reached by car. In order to camp here, however, one must comply with the can-and-bottle ban, since this place is classified as an Interior site. Because the campsite lies directly beside Barron Canyon Road, the noise from passing cars can be a drawback, although the racket generally dissipates after sunset.

WILDLIFE-VIEWING AREAS

Barron Canyon Road offers many excellent opportunities for wildlife viewing. Most of Algonquin's larger animals are often seen along the 54 kilometres of road between the gate and Lake Travers. Certain species such as porcupine, black bear and white-tailed deer are more commonly encountered here than on the Park's West Side.

Most of the following animals can be found anywhere along Barron Canyon Road. A few of the better locations for viewing each species is offered, and Chapter 3, **OBSERVING WILDLIFE**, offers tips that might increase your chances of finding these animals.

Moose

Moose can be seen between the gate and Lake Travers and are also occasionally observed along the road outside the Park. In June and early July, when moose are feeding on sodium-rich aquatic plants, the following waterways usually provide good viewing opportunities:

KM 21.4

The pond on the east side of the road is worth checking. There are a couple of short footpaths leading through the pines to the edge of the water.

KM 36.4

At this location you will find a dirt road leading off to the north (right). Although this road is closed to unauthorized vehicles, visitors are allow to walk it. About a half kilometre from Barron Canyon Road lies a beautiful pond surrounded by picturesque dead trees.

Achray Trail System — five kilometres south of KM 37.8

From the Achray turn drive five kilometres until you

reach the buildings at Achray. The Achray Trail System begins at the far end of the large parking area to your left, before the stone building, and consists of the Berm Lake Trail and the Eastern Pines Backpacking Trail. Any of portions of these trails that bring you to Berm or Johnston Lake could potentially offer views of moose. The boggy south end of Berm is particularly worth a look.

KM 44

An excellent view of the west end of a small lake is offered from this location. Occasionally I have seen moose feeding here, particularly along the opposite shore.

KM 48.3

The large pond on the south side of the road is the best summer feeding spot for moose along this road. In late June as many as 12 moose have been seen at one time. A short path leads through the pines to a fine vantage point.

Pretty Lake — KM 54.5

As its name suggests, this is a scenic lake. Moose are sometimes seen feeding along the west side of the lake.

KM 69.4

Here you will find a road leading north. As is the case with all of the Park's "closed" roads, you are permitted to walk but not drive.

After walking a little over a kilometre through a pleasant jack pine forest, you will reach the large opening where a sawmill was formerly situated. A little farther along to your left will be a short road leading to a marsh in which moose feed.

KM 72

Moose occasionally feed in the pond on your left.

White-tailed Deer

White-tailed deer are frequently seen between the gate and the Hydro Line (KM 49.9), particularly in late spring and early summer. At sunrise deer often drink at the

Black bears are relatively common on this side of the Park.

edges of ponds and streams. Thus, you might encounter them at some of the locations given above for moose. The hydro line and the abandoned mill site at Lake Travers (1.5 kilometres north from KM 69.4) are both good feeding areas.

Black Bear

There are two peak times for encountering black bears along the roadside. The first is in early spring (later April and May) when bears are seeking fresh grasses and sedges to eat. The second is in mid-summer (late mid-July to early August) when they are dining on blueberries and other fruit in open areas. Evening is the best time to look for black bears. I have had good luck in seeing these usually shy animals between KM 20 and KM 50. In particular, the following areas have been good for viewing bears:

Achray Road — KM 37.8

In late evening or around dawn bears are occasionally seen on this five-kilometre road. If you walk only a few metres into the woods along the west side of the Achray Road 0.6 to 0.8 km from where you first turned onto this road, you will find some large beech trees with excellent bear claw scars on the trunks. These were made by bears climbing the trees to get nuts in the fall.

KM 45.9

The logging road leading south has been a good area for bears in the past. If you walk a short distance up it, you will arrive at a few open areas where berry-producing plants thrive. Bears frequently forage along this road.

Hydro Line — KM 49.9

Just before the 50 KM marker, the Hydro Line crosses the Barron Canyon Road. I have seen bears here on numerous occasions, especially on the south side in summer when the berries are ripe.

Algonquin Wolves

Refer to "**Algonquin Wolves**" in **The Highway 60 Corridor** section for a discussion of these rather enigmatic animals.

I have found this part of Algonquin to offer excellent opportunities to hear, and occasionally see, wolves. Several wolf packs have territories that include parts of Barron Canyon Road. They regularly travel along the road through all seasons.

This habit of travelling provides us with important clues as to where to listen or howl. Wolf droppings are distinctive and stand out against the light colour of the sand. The droppings, also known as scats, are generally black and are full of their prey's hair. Fresh droppings look moist and won't be full of dirt from passing vehicles. On cold mornings extremely fresh scats have steam rising from them. On wet sand or fresh snow tracks are also a good clue to the presence of wolves. Whenever you encounter a fresh sign, try howling (refer to the chapter Observing Wildlife). You may be rewarded for your efforts.

Over the years I have observed wolves at the following locations:

McManus Lake Road — KM 24

Try howling at this junction. Also try approximately four kilometres down this road toward McManus Lake.

KM 30

Wolves frequently hunt in this vicinity and along the Barron River, just south of here.

Hydro Line — KM 49.9

The logging road that passes west of here is travelled by wolves, as is the road situated along the Hydro Line.

Pretty Lake — KM 54.5

This area has traditionally been good for locating wolves. I have fond memories of camping on this lake and having wolves respond from the far shore throughout the night. They also might be heard howling near Francis Lake, the lake just west of Pretty.

KM 61

A creek system lies just north where I have come across wolves a number of times.

KM 62 to KM 69

This section of road, which passes through the jack pine flats, has traditionally been one of the best wolf areas on the East Side and possibly in all of Algonquin. While you might encounter wolves anywhere along this stretch, KM 66 is the best place to stop. This point is the highest on the flats, and sound carries a phenomenally long distance to and from here.

Mill Site — 1.5 kilometres north of KM 69.4

This is another location worth trying.

Red Fox

Red foxes are usually easily located since they hunt along the roadsides, particularly at night. You might find rather tame foxes in a number of places along this route. Although the tameness is due to frequent contact with people, it is always best to be cautious and keep your distance.

KM 37.8

Since they often den near the turnoff to Achray, both adults and young are commonly seen in this vicinity from late April through summer. Foxes are frequently spotted along Achray Road, particularly the first kilometre south of the junction with Barron Canyon Road.

KM 62 to KM 72

This stretch of road passes through a sandy plateau covered in jack pine. Excellent denning sites exist in the sandbanks throughout the area. In particular the stretch of road nearest Lake Travers often affords good viewing.

Mill Site — 1.5 kilometres north from KM 69.4

Another open sandy area where foxes not only hunt but also occasionally den.

Beaver

Barron Canyon Road is excellent for observing beavers because many of the creeks and ponds along the road are occupied by these animals. Be aware that beavers periodically change sites, and that ponds occupied at time of writing may be vacant during your visit and that new colonies might arise in currently unoccupied locations. An active site will exhibit freshly cut sticks and newly placed mud on the dam or lodge. At the time of writing the following sites support active beaver colonies:

KM 21.4

The pond on the north side of the road is occupied by a colony.

Forbes Creek — KM 40

The creek crosses the road just 0.1 kilometre past this point. Beavers reside here and are occasionally seen from the road, particularly in spring.

KM 42.2 to 42.7

This stretch of Forbes Creek is worth checking.

KM 43.2

Scan for the familiar V of a beaver swimming across the lake. While spectacular sunsets are frequently viewed from this point, the next location along the lake is usually better for beaver observation.

KM 44

Beavers are commonly seen at this end of the lake in the evening.

KM 45.9

This pond was first colonized by beavers in 1992.

KM 48.3

Although this pond is better for moose viewing than for beaver watching, it is still worth checking.

KM 57

The small pond on the south side of the road was colonized in the late 1990s.

KM 72

The beaver dam is an obvious structure right along the roadside.

Otter

Because otters and beavers frequent the same habitat, virtually any of the beaver locations could produce otters. Look at those sites in addition to the ones given below. Keep in mind that smaller creeks and larger lakes are used more frequently by otters than by beavers.

Because otters range more widely than beavers, it is more difficult to predict where they might appear.

Otter activity varies seasonally. Early spring, when the ice is retreating from the waterways, and late fall are usually the best times for finding these agile animals. Some favoured otter viewing locations are:

Forbes Creek — KM 40.1

The creek crosses the road at this location and otters travel along it periodically.

KM 43.2

The bridge offers a good spot to scan both up and downstream for otters.

KM 44

An excellent view of this end of the lake is offered here.

Pretty Lake — KM 54.5

Otters regularly hunt the edges of this lake.

Lake Travers — 1.5 kilometres north from KM 69.4

Check the marsh on your left shortly after you reach the mill site. Also walk another few hundred metres to the point and carefully scan Lake Travers for these active animals.

Turtle Club Point (Lake Travers) — KM 72

For water access from the parking lot walk east on the footpath starting behind the bulletin board. This route takes you to a point where the magnificent Turtle Club lodge once stood. Only a few piles of rubble and five stark chimneys remain to mark the site of the buildings.

This point offers excellent views of the Petawawa River and the south end of Lake Travers. Otters hunt for fish and crayfish throughout the year here, but early spring and late fall are the best seasons to look. At these times the strong current keeps the water open at the mouth of the river while the lake remains frozen. Otters bring their catch onto the edge of the ice, using it as a dining table.

You should also check the pond on the south side of the road at KM 72. just beyond the KM 72 sign, the bridge over the Petawawa offers another vantage point from which to look.

BIRDS

As in the section on birds in Chapter 5, The Highway Corridor, the northern species frequently sought by birders are detailed. In addition, a few locations for other species of interest are provided. Tips on locating particular species as well as attracting birds in general are given in Chapter 3, **OBSERVING WILDLIFE**.

Spruce Grouse

While this bird is found in and near spruce bogs on the western side of Algonquin, on the East Side it is also found in jack pine forests. This species is actually more frequent here and is often observed, particularly shortly

Spruce Grouse can frequently be seen on road edges near Lake Travers

after sunrise and in late afternoon, picking grit from the road. Also, Spruce Grouse are commonly seen feeding in the pines along the road, especially in winter. If not seen on the road, they are sometimes discovered by walking through the jack pines. The following locations have consistently produced Spruce Grouse:

KM 61.5 to KM 62

The black spruce/tamarack bog on the south side of the road is worth checking.

KM 63 to KM 63.5

The south side of the road, particularly the black spruce edge, is a regular spot.

KM 65 to KM 70

Spruce Grouse are common throughout these jack pine flats. In particular the pines near the Stuart Spur junction at KM 67 and along the stretch between KM 67.5 and KM 69.4 usually harbour grouse.

North from KM 69.4

I have found Spruce Grouse on numerous occasions by walking the 1.5-kilometre road that leads north to the old mill site on Lake Travers.

Gray Jay

Gray jays can be spotted on this side of the Park but, unlike the birds found along Highway 60, they lack coloured bands on their legs. However, they will still approach you for food, so be sure to have a chunk of bread or some other offering when you come across these gentle birds. Gray Jays are fairly common over much of this side of the Park, and a few of the more regular places for them are given here.

McManus Lake Road — KM 24

This eight-kilometre road frequently has Gray Jays at various points along it.

Barron Canyon Trail — KM 28.9

Gray Jays are regularly spotted along the trail, but the parking lot is as one of the better places to see them.

Achray Turn — KM 37.8

Gray Jays are often viewed at this junction.

Forbes Creek — KM 40.1

This boreal stretch commonly produces jays.

Pretty Lake — KM 54.5

Usually there is a family group not far from the campsite along the road.

KM 62.2

Anywhere near the creek is a good place to look for this species.

Whitson Creek — KM 63.7

This is one of the better spots for finding these and other northern birds.

KM 65 to KM 72

The jack pine flats support a number of Gray Jays.

North from KM 69.4

The road to the mill site and the periphery of the open area, particularly near the marsh, usually has Gray Jays.

Black-backed Woodpecker

This northern woodpecker is frequently spotted on the East Side of Algonquin. I have encountered this species throughout most of this region, including along both interpretive trails and all along Barron Canyon Road. Black-backed Woodpeckers might be found in any of the pine forests along this road. Some of the more regular locations for this bird include:

McManus Road — KM 24

One of the better spots on this generally good road is the black spruce bog that lies on the east (right) side of the road approximately one kilometre north of Barron Canyon Road.

KM 35.2

The dead trees along the creek are worth checking.

KM 37

The wet spruce/fir area can be good for these northern birds.

Pretty Lake — KM 54.5

KM 61.5 to KM 62.2

Whitson Creek — KM 63.7

Although the area along the southeast side of the road is often productive, Black-backed Woodpeckers might be found anywhere near the creek.

KM 65 to KM 72

North from KM 69.4

This road, closed to vehicles, often provides encounters with this species.

OTHER SPECIES

Because of the pine/poplar forests certain species of birds are more easily found on this side of Algonquin than in the west. In particular Pine Warblers, Dark-eyed Juncos and Pileated Woodpeckers are quite common. A few additional species, including some of the East Side specialities, are discussed below.

Red Crossbill

Because of the abundance of white pines, their preferred seed tree, Red Crossbills are usually present year-round. Some years they occur in large numbers all along Barron

Canyon Road and frequently pick grit from its surface. In years of lower populations two relatively good spots are the Sand Lake Gate and the Turtle Club site east of KM 72. At the latter location Red Crossbills are often found gleaning lime from the chimneys, particularly during late fall through spring.

Merlin

These agile falcons are fairly common on the East Side. One pair usually resides near Achray and occasionally chases swallows near the boat launch.

The Lake Travers area usually supports several pairs of Merlins. They are frequently seen either perching on the tops of dead snags or flying over the jack pine flats, especially between KM 63 and KM 71.5. One pair usually nests at the old mill site (1.5 kilometres north of KM 69.4) and also hunts at the Turtle Club site (on the point east of the parking lot at KM 72).

Barred Owl

While perhaps not quite as common as they are along the Highway Corridor, Barred Owls can be heard on the East Side at a number of locations.

Barron Canyon Trail — KM 28.9

I have heard owls not only from the vicinity of the parking lot but also from the top of the trail.

KM 37

This is one of the traditional spots from where I have heard Barred Owls at night, particularly just before the break of dawn.

Maple Forest on Achray Road — 1.2 kilometres south from KM 37.8

This mature stand of hardwoods, one of the only stands along public roads on the East Side, invariably has a pair of Barred Owls residing in it.

Whip-poor-will and Common Nighthawk

Both of these birds are much more easily encountered on the East Side than along Highway 60. Nighthawks start hunting before dusk and are fairly easy to see. Their raspy "peent" calls and booming courtship sounds identify their whereabouts. Whip-poor-wills are also easy to hear but are generally much tougher to see. However, they frequently sit on sandy roads and their eyes glow bright red in headlight beams. Thus, a slow drive in the right areas might produce a view of these tough-to-see birds.

Both species can be heard at Grand Lake, but the best area lies in the jack pine flats between KM 64 and KM 67 (KM 66 is the optimal location). Try listening around dusk or just before sunrise.

OTHER HIGHLIGHTS

Because the topography and soils are different than those of western Algonquin, flora and fauna occur that are unique to the East Side. Several phenomena in particular are noteworthy.

A healthy population of wood turtles, a rare reptile throughout North America, exists along the Petawawa River. These turtles are distinctive, possessing an ornate shell and orange front legs and throat. During the egg-laying season in early June, they are occasionally seen crossing Barron Canyon Road near the Lake Travers of the same name. They are also seen along the Petawawa River. If you are fortunate enough to encounter a wood turtle, please don't disturb it.

Another turtle found on this side of the Park and occasionally confused with wood turtles is Blanding's turtle. This species, however, has a bright yellow throat and smooth, spotted shell.

In late May and early June in even-numbered years the Macoun's Arctic, a boreal butterfly that appears every two years, flies in the larger jack pine stands near Lake Travers. It is pale orange and resembles a small washed-out monarch butterfly. Algonquin Park represents the southernmost range in Ontario of this butterfly.

Another noteworthy East Side phenomenon is the spectacular late summer show of wildflowers along the rivers, particularly at Poplar Rapids on the Petawawa River (KM 72.1). From late July to mid-August the edges of the Petawawa (and, in places, the Barron River) flame with the vibrant red blossoms of cardinal-flower. The small island just upstream from the bridge over Poplar Rapids annually exhibits one of the most exquisite wildflower gardens I have ever seen. Here the soft pink of joe-pye weed, the yellow of grass-leaved golden-rod, the white of boneset and the crimson of cardinal-flower all blend to create a symphony of colour.

HISTORICAL POINTS OF INTEREST

The East Side of Algonquin was one of the first to feel the logger's axe because of the rich supply of pines that grew here and also because of its closeness to the Ottawa Valley, the hub of lumbering activity in eastern Ontario. The Petawawa River was extremely important in the transport of logs from the Park to the Ottawa River, and every spring swarms of men moved thousands of logs down its length. The last log drive in Algonquin Park took place on this river in 1959.

Because of its rugged beauty this side of Algonquin also attracted the attention of renowned artists. Tom Thomson not only sketched some of his most famous works on the East Side but also worked here as a fire ranger in the summer of 1916.

McManus Blowdown — 6 kilometres north from KM 24

On July 5, 1999, a severe wind storm known as a microburst touched down in the McManus Lake area. The winds snapped off pines and other trees as if they were matchsticks. The dramatic effects of the wind can be viewed at several locations along the two-kilometre section of road between Frontier Lake and the boat launch on McManus Lake. The aftermath of the storm can also be seen on the far shore of McManus directly across the boat launch.

Several other sites showing the effects of that wind include KM 50 (just west of the hydro line), KM 54.7 (west end of Pretty Lake), and the northwest corner of the mill site at Lake Travers (1.5 km north of KM 69.4)

Logging Camp Remains — KM 31.6

A boggy pond lies on the south side of the road. On the northwest side of this wetland you will find the remnants of a logging camp, which was built in the 1930s by a contractor for the Whitmore Lumber Company. An old well, foundations and assorted camp debris are present. The ruins of an older camp, probably a camboose, are also located here.

Pine Forest Research Area — KM 36.4

A research project on the dynamics of white pine growth was conducted here in 1929. A joint venture between the Department of Lands and Forests (now the Ministry of Natural Resources) and the University of Toronto, the study was the first of its kind in Ontario. Trees bearing numbered tags from this program can be found in proximity to the junction of Barron Canyon Road and the logging road running north. The trees were measured again in 1949, but no further examination occurred until the 1980s.

CNR Rail Bed — five kilometres south of KM 37.8

As you enter Achray, you cross the abandoned Canadian National Railway line. This line was built through Algonquin between 1912 and 1915 by the Canadian Northern Railway. In 1918, Canadian Northern Railway was purchased by Canadian National Railway. The railway line ran under this latter name until 1995, when service was rerouted outside the Park onto the Canadian Pacific Railway line. The last train through Algonquin was Train No. 114 on November 25, 1995. The steel rails and wooden ties were removed from the Park in 1996 and 1997. You can also access the rail bed at Stuart's Spur and KM 70.3 (discussed later in this section).

This stone building is still used as the headquarters for the eastern side of the Park.

Stone Building at Achray — five kilometres south from KM 37.8

As you enter Achray, a large stone building lies directly ahead on Grand Lake. The building, erected in 1933 as an office for this part of Algonquin, was constructed with stone hauled from across the lake. It continues to be used as the headquarters for the East Side.

The Out-Side-In Cabin — Achray

This structure, used as a fire ranger's cabin in the early 1900s, is located just east of the stone building. Tom Thomson lived here in the summer of 1916 when he worked as a fire ranger. During his stay, he painted a sign bearing this unusual name. Unfortunately the original sign's whereabouts are currently unknown, but a replica is to be erected on the cabin.

Site of Tom Thomson's *The Jack Pine* — Grand Lake

Tom Thomson's famous painting was sketched in 1916 from a point just south of the Achray Campground. To reach this site travel along the road through the east end of the campground until you come to a small parking lot. From here continue by foot along the road through a chain gate and across a short causeway. If this part of the road is underwater, as it can be at times, you can skirt around it by travelling along the abandoned railway bed to your left. The road continues through a mixed woods to a rocky ridge on the right. Here a trail leads you up the hill through some jack pines. When you stand on the top of this rocky knoll, face the delightful rolling hills surrounding Carcajou Bay, southwest across the lake. The jack pine is gone, but the rolling hills that appear in the painting's background easily identify this as the site of the famous work of art.

Ranke Sawmill Site and Log Chute — 0.4 kilometre north of KM 38.3

Walk up the road leading north from Lake Travers Road. A short distance in you will reach a gravel pit around which remnants of the Ranke Sawmill are situated. This mill was built, as many mills and logging camps were, on the site of a much older camp.

Just beyond the pit is Forbes Creek. Walk downstream approximately 100 metres or less to a small rapids. The flat planks along the creek are from the bottom of a log chute that once carried logs past these rapids.

Blowdown — KM 50

The downed trees on both sides of the road are the result of the July 5, 1999 windstorm that also created the McManus Blowdown.

Blowdown — KM 54.7

More evidence of the severe windstorm of July 5, 1999 can be seen just past the west end of Pretty Lake.

Stuart's Spur — 0.5 kilometre south from KM 67

Stuart was the manager of the Pembroke Shook Mills, which built a loading spur — a short section of rail —

126

here in 1929. At this spur joining the now-abandoned Canadian National Railway line pine logs were loaded onto flatcars by a steam hoist. The high ground around the small parking area just north of Travers Creek once held a number of buildings, including a stable, blacksmith shop, cookery and bunkhouses. The alder flats between the high ground and the now abandoned CNR Railway line was the holding area for pine logs destined for the shook mills in Pembroke. (Shooks were prefab wooden boxes.) A dam on Travers Creek kept the holding area flooded to prevent logs from staining due to exposure to the air before they were loaded for transport. The camp lasted until 1954.

A more recent camp was run by Shaw Lumber on the opposite side of the rail bed in the vicinity of the large clearing. In order to transport the logs from this site the railway spur was moved to that side of the former tracks. High quality red pine logs had their bark peeled before they were shipped for use as telephone, hydro or utility poles. Lower-grade red and white pine logs were shipped directly to the Pembroke Shook Mills. This camp shut down in the late 1960s but was briefly opened for the 1980-81 season. In 1988 the camp was completely dismantled and the spur area planted.

Don't be surprised if you see horse hoof prints or even horses on this road. Access by this method is allowed along the road to White Partridge Lake.

In 1999, high spring water washed out the culvert on Travers Creek. Thus, if you wish to visit the Shaw Lumber camp site, unless the culvert has been replaced you must either ford the creek or walk along the abandoned CNR rail bed. The rail bed can be accessed by driving 0.8 kilometre south from KM 70.3. Here a side road branches off to the left. Park and walk along this very short left branch (closed to vehicles) until you reach the rail bed. Turn left (east) and walk approximately four kilometres along the rail bed until you reach the large open area on your right.

Pembroke Lumber Company Mill Site — 1.5 kilometres north from KM 69.4

Park safely off the main road and walk 1.5 kilometres north along the side road to a large opening, the site of a mill run by the Pembroke Lumber Company. Built in the early 1930s, it ran until 1977, a phenomenal length of time for an isolated mill in Algonquin. Not much remains today except for debris scattered here and there. The most obvious remaining structure is a small water tower to your left when you approach the lake. The broken trees around the water tower are a result of the wind storm that took place July 5, 1999.

CNR Railway Bed- 2 km south of KM 70.3

When you drive south on this road, keep to the right when you reach a fork 0.8 km from the main road. You eventually reach the rail bed. Several small buildings, including a small station house, formerly stood on the far side of rail bed, to the right of the pond. The buildings were taken down shortly after the railway line was removed.

Radio Observatory — KM 70.3 and KM 71.5

This area was set aside in 1959 for the National Research Council (NRC), and returned to provincial jurisdiction in 1996. While much of the original operation has been shut down, a large radio telescope, known as the "Big Dish," is still used to search for radio signals from outer space. The Big Dish is located on the private road leading west from KM 70.5 but can be partially viewed by looking west past the pond at KM 72. An inactive bank of smaller dishes, formerly used for solar observation, can be seen 0.3 kilometre along the road south from KM 70.3. These are currently being dismantled. The research complex, last manned by NRC in the late 1980s, was operated for a number of ensuing years by the Institute for Space and Terrestrial Science (ISTS). From 1991 to 1993, ISTS also held a Space

Camp at this site. At the time of writing, the complex is now operated by Natural Resources Canada (NRCan).

Turtle Club Site — 0.2 kilometre north from KM 72

Park in the lot for water access to the lake and look for the footpath that starts from behind the information board. The path leads to the point where the Turtle Club was situated. Erected in 1933, the club was a private lodge owned by the family of J.R. Booth, the famous lumber baron. Five chimneys plus a pile of debris mark the site where the unique structure formerly stood. The elegant log building was constructed in the shape of a turtle, Booth's bark mark (a symbol inscribed on the side of logs to identify the owner). Purchased by the government in 1973, the building was dismantled five years later.

Only the chimneys remain to mark the site of the magnificent Turtle Club.

Glance Piers — KM 72.1

If you stand on the bridge over Poplar Rapids and look upstream, you will see piers of piled rocks jutting into the Petawawa River. Probably built well before the turn of the century, these rock piles kept logs away from the shoreline and directed them into the channel during spring river drives. For over 100 years the Petawawa River carried logs from Algonquin Park to the Ottawa River. The last log drive in the Park took place on this river in 1959.

CANOEING ON THE EAST SIDE

Although fewer in number, the canoe routes here are often more dramatic than those in the Highway Corridor. Another major difference is that fabulous white-water canoeing is available for those who seek it. The Petawawa River is renowned for this feature, but only people with experience should attempt to "shoot" (canoe) the rapids." Highly recommended for canoeing this river is the *Petawawa River Whitewater Guide*, produced by The Friends of Algonquin Park. *The Canoe Routes of Algonquin Provincial Park* map brochure shows the campsites and location of the rapids and the portages that bypass them, but does not go into the detail of the *Petawawa River Whitewater Guide*.

Available Services

There are no rental services on the East Side. However, the Algonquin Portage Store, which is 21 kilometres outside the gate, offers complete outfitting and shuttle services.

Recommended Short Trips

The following are all short excursions, one day or less, that could be extended into longer trips if desired. Remember, cans and bottles are prohibited in the Interior and camping permits are required for overnight stays. *The Canoe Routes of Algonquin Provincial Park* map brochure is essential for any canoe trip in the Park.

The Barron Canyon is as impressive from below as it is from the trail at the top.

Barron River

The 100-metre-high cliffs of Barron Canyon make canoeing the Barron River an awe-inspiring event. The river can be accessed from Squirrel Rapids (KM 20.3) or from the Brigham Lake Access (KM 33.2). Both sites have parking facilities. The Brigham Lake Access is closer to the canyon but has a steeper access to the water. From Squirrel Rapids to the canyon you are paddling against the gentle current, but on the return trip you are, not surprisingly, travelling with it. One enjoyable way of doing this route is to travel in two parties. One vehicle can be dropped off at Squirrel Rapids, making the trip a one-way excursion from the Brigham Lake Access. Be aware that there are four portages on the route (the longest 440 m), three upstream and one downstream of the canyon.

When you journey through the canyon, you are travelling back in time. Birds that usually nest on man-made structures can be seen nesting on these cliffs as they have done for countless thousands of years. When you paddle along the sheer wall of rock, watch for the mud nests of Barn Swallows cemented under overhangs at about eye level. Flowing streams of excrement below the nests identify their location. As you near active nests, the adult birds noisily dive-bomb your canoe. Eastern Phoebes, less aggressive birds, also share the same recesses, but their nests have more moss and lichen components than those of Barn Swallows.

Higher up on the cliff faces, the bulky stick nests of Common Ravens can also be seen. From the tops of the cliffs Red-tailed Hawks indignantly scream at your intrusion into their domain.

The cliff faces are also adorned with a variety of intriguing plants. Plants from the far north remain as tokens of the cold past. Many thrive here because of the lime that percolates from rock crevices. Because lime is rare throughout most of Algonquin, a number of the plants you pass by are unique to the canyon. The lichen Xanthoria is responsible for the beautiful orange that carpets much of the exposed rock. Another plant to look for is the encrusted saxifrage, easily identified because of the white dots of lime exuded around the periphery of the leaves, which grow in a basal rosette.

The roar of the river is now silenced, as is the thunder of log drives that occurred here in more recent times. The Barron River was an important route for spring drives, and countless thousands of logs passed through here from the mid-1800s to the early 1900s. The grave of one unfortunate driver lies along the river at the second camp-site below the canyon, hidden by a clump of conifers.

Along the river you will find old logs left behind from these drives. Check the ends carefully for the log stamp of J.R. Booth, the great lumber baron who brought the OA & PS Railway to Algonquin. The stamp was a diamond with the initials J.R. inside it.

The indistinct ruins of a log chute can be found at Cache Rapids, the first set of rapids upstream from Squirrel Rapids.

Grand Lake

Despite the presence of motorboats (up to 10-horse-power motors are allowed), Grand Lake remains a marvellous body of water to paddle. Several options exist as to where you can go and what you can see on a day's paddle from Achray, five kilometres south from KM 37.8.

Option 1 — Grand Lake. A full day can be spent paddling to the lake's northwest extremity and back. I would allow a minimum of eight hours for this, so you should start at dawn to ensure plenty of time for exploring.

With its narrow configuration Grand Lake is more like a river than a lake. Two points of interest lie along this route. Approximately halfway up the lake, on the west side, is the portage to Wenda Lake. Discarded mechanical items and an old root cellar can be found near the start of the portage. These identify the site of a former lumber camp.

The remains of the McLachlin Depot, a central supply settlement for lumbering operations in the area, are located at the north end of the large bay at the north-east corner of the lake. At one time logs were hauled overland on wooden rails by a steam locomotive with double-flange wheels, then deposited in Grand Lake.

At the very top end of the lake lies one of the few cattail marshes in Algonquin. Here Great Blue Herons and American Bitterns stalk frogs along the narrow creek that meanders through the marsh. If you are fortunate, you might startle a Virginia Rail into uttering its alarm call, a weird *wugh-wugh-wugh-wugh-wugh* that sounds like a giant coin wobbling to a halt after being spun on a tabletop. These secretive birds also emit a sharp *dik-dik-kidik-kidik*. The Grand Lake marsh supports the highest density of Virginia Rails in the Park.

Across the logging road at the north end of the marsh lies Clemow Lake, the beautiful body of water depicted in the coniferous forest diorama in the Algonquin Visitor Centre. A lumber camp formerly stood at the north end of this lake at the site of the northernmost campsite.

Option 2 — Carcajou Bay. Carcajou is a French word that means "wolverine." Although these large weasels are not currently known in the Park, the use of this word in naming a bay, a lake and a creek suggests that perhaps at one time they were here.

It is the hills from the bay region that form the backdrop for Tom Thomson's *The Jack Pine*, painted from the Achray side. The route is a beautiful one that should be done well after black fly season ends. The East Side is notoriously bad for these biting creatures during June, and the Carcajou area seems to hold the highest population in the world!

After leaving Achray, a relatively short paddle brings you across the lake. Before entering the bay you pass by an island with a Herring Gull colony on it. At times the gulls have an intriguing method of nest defence — they fly over your canoe and either vomit rotting fish or defecate on you. Thus, I suggest you give the island a wide berth.

Once in the "safety" of the bay, carefully check the rocks on your right (the north side). Indian pictographs are situated just above eye level on the low cliffs immediately after you enter the bay. These are quite faded but still discernible. I have found that by splashing water on them the symbols become more visible.

The dramatic rocky hills bordering Carcajou Bay make this a particularly enjoyable route. A delightful waterfall is situated at the south end of the bay. After one short portage, you have the choice of taking another short portage and canoeing into Lower Spectacle Lake or continuing up McDonald Creek, a winding bog-lined waterway and an excellent moose area in the summer.

Option 3 — Stratton Lake. After leaving Achray, paddle along the south shore of the lake, past the extensive sand beaches where native people once camped. Soon after entering the narrows you will reach a short portage skirting the dam. Stratton Lake lies on the far side of the portage. It is a beautiful rock-bound body of water that seems more like a narrow river than an actual lake.

Ospreys and otters are frequently seen as they search for fish in the clear waters. Since this was an important waterway for log drives in earlier years, evidence of that activity abounds.

Once at the south end of the lake you have the choice of taking a 45-metre portage into St. Andrew's Lake or paddling to the end of the bay that runs north from here. I would suggest you do both, but obviously not at the same time! High Falls, a thundering waterfall, lies at the end of the north-running bay, and the remains of a logging camp are situated on the extreme northern tip.

St. Andrew's Lake provides access to a couple of fascinating relics from early logging days. A pointer boat, a logging vessel narrowed at both ends, lies at the bottom of the lake at its northern extremity, just before the portage and closer to the far shore. If the water surface is not ruffled by wind, you should be able to see it by peering into the water.

Another fascinating bit of history lies along the portage into Highfalls Lake. The remnants of the wooden log chute used to transport logs around the rapids along the portage are still apparent. The best section lies between the pond approximately halfway along the portage and the end of the portage at Highfalls Lake.

Because the chute lies on the far side of the rapids, which the portage parallels, you may wish to walk along that side to view it. After you finish the portage to Highfalls Lake, you can paddle to the opposite shore and walk back up the rapids.

From here, if time permits, you can travel on to Barron Canyon, but several small portages must be traversed to get there. If two parties are involved, one vehicle could be left at either Brigham Lake or Squirrel Rapids Access. Be sure if you do a one-way trip that you start early in the day to avoid paddling in the dark.

The ruins of an early logging camp can be seen along the portage between Opalescent and Ooze lakes, and the remains of a cabin, possibly a river drivers' shelter, lie halfway along the 285-metre portage between Ooze and The Cascades.

Lake Travers

This, my favourite lake in Algonquin, offers excellent canoeing. However, on windy days Travers can be rough, so keep abreast of the weather situation while on it.

There is a parking lot and boat launch at KM 72. Here you launch directly into the Petawawa River. As you paddle along, you are following the route of the early river drivers. The point on your right bearing tall chimneys is the site of the Turtle Club, described in **Historical Points of Interest** in this chapter.

If you paddle east around the south edge of the lake, you will pass below a few buildings associated with the Radio Observatory complex. Beyond these lies an interesting marsh. Here you will likely see Great Blue Herons and American Bitterns. At daybreak the marsh is full of life. I have seen deer, raccoons, moose, muskrats, otters and beavers in this terrific marsh, as well as rare visitors such as Black-crowned Night Heron and Snowy Egret.

From here you paddle north past the old mill site with the remnants of a dock and other buildings along the rocky point. Beyond there lies a shallow bay with a long sand beach. Farther north the scenery becomes more dramatic as steep hills embrace the lake where it narrows back into a river.

The large island just before the narrows is a moose-calving spot in mid-May and usually harbours nesting Merlins. A point bearing an old logging camp lies about half a kilometre beyond the small island and campsites in the narrows. The site is on the west side of the river and is hidden by alders. About another three kilometres past this you will see that the hillside to the right of you has had most of the trees knocked down. This blow-down occurred during a windstorm in 1983. just beyond that spot lies the portage around Big Thomson Rapids. Remnants of a wooden logging dam are quite evident near the start of the portage. Unless you are planning to continue down the Petawawa on an overnight excursion, this portage will be the place where you turn back.

McManus, Smith and Whitson lakes

These so-called lakes are simply widenings in the Petawawa River. To access McManus take the well-marked road at KM 24. The parking lot and water access lie eight kilometres from the turn.

On the first leg of this trip you paddle against a gentle current. There are only two small portages along the route, the first a mere 90 metres in length. If the water is high enough and you have the strength, the first portage can be bypassed by paddling up the rapids. But believe me, this is tough work and the portage is a considerably easier option.

While these lakes offer pleasant canoeing, the landscape is less varied than along the other routes. This route does, however, have some interesting tree species. Along the shores one finds green alder, a much rarer shrub in the Park than its abundant relative, speckled alder. Green alder has sticky young leaves and branchlets, and the conelike catkins are held on long stalks. Speckled alders have dry leaves and branchlets and short-stalked catkins.

On the small islands in Whitson Lake silver maple will also be found. This southern tree is quite rare in Algonquin except along the Petawawa River. The leaves of this maple are very deeply cut in contrast to those of its relatives. From the islands the rising song of Warbling Vireos, a southern species irregular and rare elsewhere in the Park, can be heard.

The return trip is virtually effortless, since you are travelling with the current all the way.

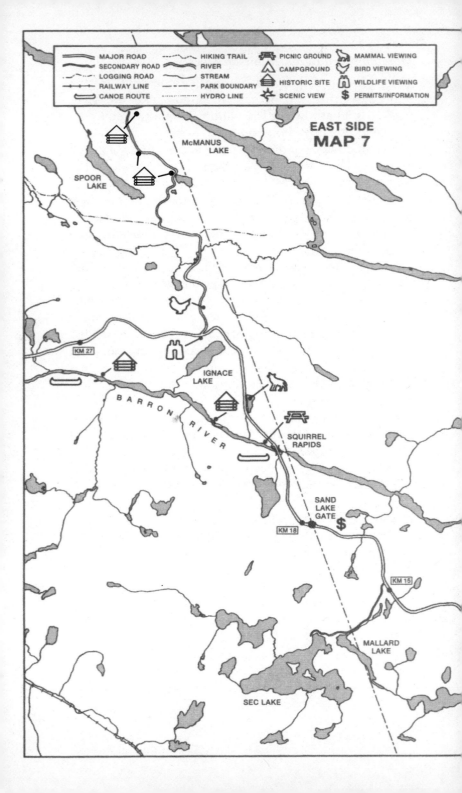

LEGEND

MAJOR ROAD	HIKING TRAIL	PICNIC GROUND	MAMMAL VIEWING
SECONDARY ROAD	RIVER	CAMPGROUND	BIRD VIEWING
LOGGING ROAD	STREAM	HISTORIC SITE	WILDLIFE VIEWING
RAILWAY LINE	PARK BOUNDARY	SCENIC VIEW	PERMITS/INFORMATION
CANOE ROUTE	HYDRO LINE		$

EAST SIDE
MAP 7

McMANUS LAKE

SPOOR LAKE

KM 27

IGNACE LAKE

BARRON RIVER

SQUIRREL RAPIDS

SAND LAKE GATE

KM 18

$

KM 15

MALLARD LAKE

SEC LAKE

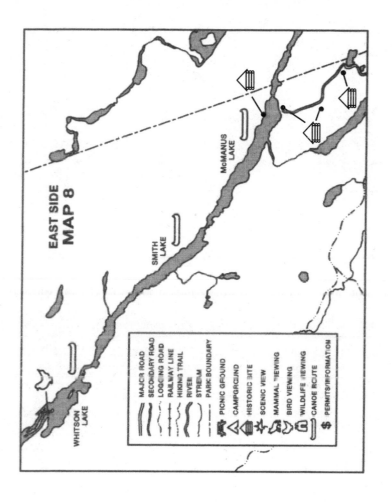

EAST SIDE
MAP 8

WHITSON
LAKE

SMITH
LAKE

McMANUS
LAKE

MAJOR ROAD
SECONDARY ROAD
LOGGING ROAD
RAILWAY LINE
HIKING TRAIL
RIVER
STREAM
PARK BOUNDARY
PICNIC GROUND
CAMPGROUND
HISTORIC SITE
SCENIC VIEW
MAMMAL VIEWING
BIRD VIEWING
WILDLIFE VIEWING
CANOE ROUTE
$ PERMITS/INFORMATION

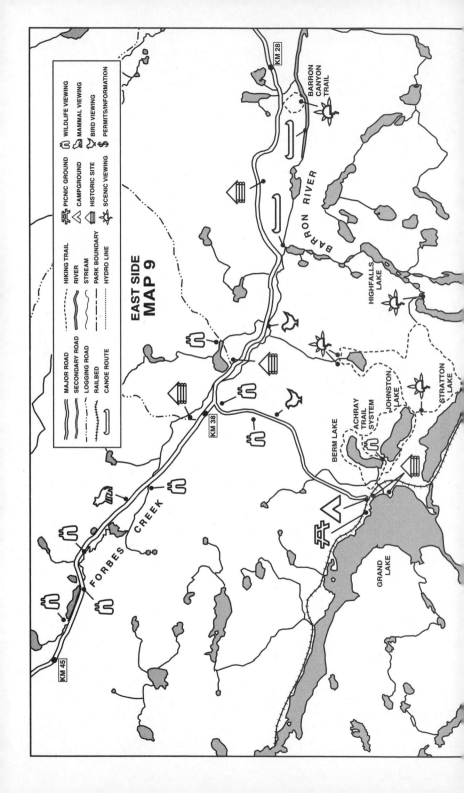

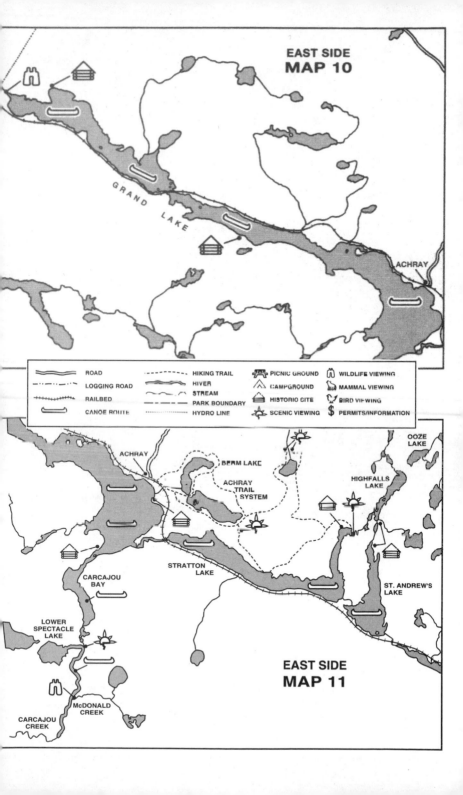

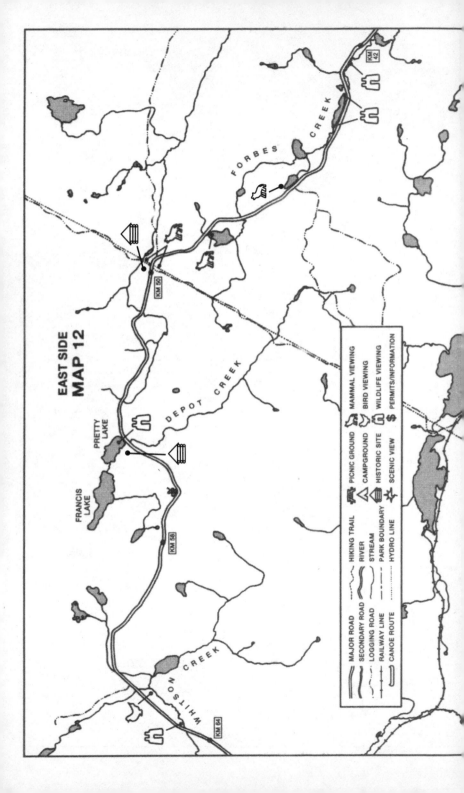

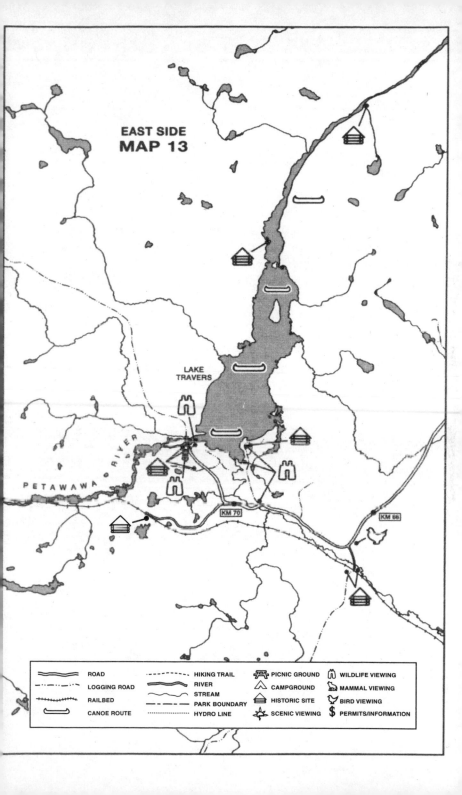

EAST SIDE
MAP 13

LAKE
TRAVERS

PETAWAWA RIVER

KM 70

KM 66

	ROAD		HIKING TRAIL	PICNIC GROUND		WILDLIFE VIEWING
	LOGGING ROAD		RIVER	CAMPGROUND		MAMMAL VIEWING
	RAILBED		STREAM	HISTORIC SITE		BIRD VIEWING
	CANOE ROUTE		PARK BOUNDARY	SCENIC VIEWING	$	PERMITS/INFORMATION
			HYDRO LINE			

This south-east section of Algonquin remains one of the least used, which is rather surprising because it possesses a wealth of animal life, fascinating historic sites, and its own special beauty. While at the time of writing there are no interpretive or hiking trails, many other options are available to the visitor. For the camper, a number of drive-in campsites are situated on water, and most of these are available through summer and fall. As an alternative to these Interior campsites, another Provincial Park offering full services lies within a 15 minute drive from the Algonquin Park entrance. Bonnechere Provincial Park is not only a stone's throw away; a number of that park's special programs are held in the Basin Depot region of Algonquin. Annual Public

The picturesque Bonnechere River is more of a creek in this part of Algonquin.

Wolf Howls and an archaeology program (which has involved archaeological digs) are offered.

The Basin Depot area possesses a long history of logging and sparse settlement. Logging began in the Bonnechere Valley before 1830. The Bonnechere River, which the road roughly parallels, was previously used for log transport during spring drives. In the summer months this meandering waterway becomes more of a creek and, for much of its length, isn't traversable by canoe. Basin Depot, a supply base and stopover spot for lumbermen, was the centre of logging activity between the mid-1800s and 1913. One of the buildings, repaired in recent years by the Algonquin Forestry Authority, is the oldest building in the Park.

Basin Road is unpaved and stretches 25 kilometres from the Park boundary to the end of public access at the Hydro Line. There are three short side branches you can take by vehicle. Two take you to lakes (Basin and Foys) while the third brings you to a beautiful section of the Bonnechere River.

Although there are no facilities along this road, the area is still worth visiting for the wildlife and historical sites. Every kilometre of main road is marked with kilometre signs, as is the case along the Highway Corridor and Barron Canyon Road.

The marking system for this road begins at the intersection with a north-leading road two kilometres west of Turner's Camp. The Park boundary lies 8.5 kilometres west of this junction, halfway between the KM 8 and KM 9 markers. This will be designated as KM 8.5. Basin Depot is situated at KM 14.2.

Access to this part of Algonquin is achieved by travelling west on Turner's Road from Highway 62, just north of the entrance into Bonnechere Provincial Park. Turner's Road is approximately 40 kilometres west of Pembroke.

The Basin Depot region supports pine and poplar forests that are representative of the entire northeastern two-thirds of the Park. In addition, jack pines are prevalent in several areas, particularly near the Park boundary and in the vicinity of the Hydro Line. These forests support a variety of wildlife, including a large population of white-tailed deer and beaver. In turn these animals support several packs of wolves, which are often heard at the appropriate times of year.

There are no campgrounds in this part of Algonquin, but there are a number of drive-in Interior sites. There are four situated at Basin Lake (1.5 km north of KM 14.2), three at Foys Lake (4 km north of KM 23.6), two on the Bonnechere River (1.2 km south of KM 30.6), one on Little Norway Lake (KM 31.1), and one at the Hydro Line where it meets the Bonnechere River (KM 33.8). These can be reserved through the Provincial Park Reservations number (1-800-ONT-PARK) or through Turner's Camp (1-613-757-2672), on a first-come,first-served basis. Turner's Camp, which lies 4.6 kilometres west of Highway 62 and 10.5 kilometres east of the Algonquin Park boundary, also offers cabins, campsites outside Algonquin, Park permits and publications, and snacks.

If you prefer a campground that offers full services, Bonnechere Provincial Park is a perfect option. Not only does this Park have its own interpretive program, it also offers archaeological digs and Public Wolf Howls in the Basin Depot region of Algonquin. Contact Bonnechere for more information (613-757-2103).

WILDLIFE-VIEWING AREAS

Because the forest type is similar to that on the East Side of Algonquin, many of the same plants and animals are found in the Basin Depot area. The road passes by several ponds and other small waterways that present opportunities to view animals such as otters and beavers. Porcupines are relatively common due to the abundance of poplars. A few of the better spots for specific animals are given below. Chapter 3, **Observing Wildlife** provides suggestions for finding these and other animals.

Moose sometimes frequent the Bonnechere River near the Hydro Line.

Moose

Although they might be encountered anywhere along the road, moose are seen more regularly in early summer when feeding on the sodium-rich aquatic plants in waterways along the road. A few of the better locations are given here.

- Pond — KM 19.5.
- Pond — KM 27.6. This has traditionally been one of the "hot spots" for moose.
- Wetland — KM 30.8.
- Pond and creek — KM 31.1.
- Bonnechere River — KM 32.2.
- Bonnechere River at Hydro Line — KM 34.2.

White-tailed Deer

The entire area is good for deer. Thus, they might be encountered anywhere along the road. The large openings around Basin Depot (KM 14.2) are often productive.

Black Bear

Another animal that might be seen anywhere along the main road, black bears frequently forage along the hydro line at the northern extremity of Basin Road.

Algonquin Wolves

This road transects one of the better areas for wolf activity because of the abundance of deer and beavers, their principal prey. When fresh signs (i.e., tracks or scats) are encountered along the road, howling attempts (see Chapter 3, **OBSERVING WILDLIFE**) should be made.

Public Wolf Howls are held in this part of Algonquin on the third Saturday of August each year. While the slide presentation is given in Bonnechere Provincial Park the howling is done in the Basin Depot area. I lead the event and plans are to expand the program into the fall. Contact Bonnechere Park for more details (613-757-2103).

Wolves can be encountered anywhere on the Basin Road but a few of the better locations for hearing (and potentially seeing) them are:

- Park Boundary — KM 8.5
- Basin Depot — KM 14.2
- Foys Lake turn — KM 23.6
- Bonnechere River — 1.2 km south of KM 30.6
- Little Norway Lake — KM 31.1
- Bonnechere River — KM 32.2
- Hydro Line — KM 33.8

Beaver

Beavers are quite common along this road. At the time of writing the following waterways are occupied by beavers:

- KM 19.5.
- One kilometre north from KM 23.6 (Foys Lake turn).
- KM 24.4
- KM 26.
- KM 27.6.
- KM 29.6.
- KM 30.8.

Otter

Because otters travel widely their whereabouts are not as predictable as those of beavers. However, they are frequently encountered in ponds and creeks along Basin Road. Any of the locations for beavers and moose might produce otters. In addition, the creek along the north side of the road from KM 20.8 to KM 21 is particularly good for otter activity.

BIRDS

The pine and poplar forests support birds similar to those on the East Side. Gray Jays are often viewed along Basin Road, as are Black-backed Woodpeckers, another northern species. Pileated Woodpeckers are also quite common.

Gray Jay and Black-backed Woodpecker

Because of the prevalence of northern coniferous forests around wetlands along Basin Road, both these northern birds are fairly common. While they may be encountered almost anywhere, there are a few locations that may offer better opportunities in seeing one or both species.

- Park Boundary — KM 8.5.
- Basin Depot — KM 14.2.
- KM 21.6.
- KM 24 to KM 26.
- KM 30.8 to KM 31.1.
- Bonnechere River — KM 32.2.

HISTORICAL POINTS OF INTEREST

Because of early settlement and the area's importance to the logging industry, Basin Road is richly endowed with historical sites. The earliest settlers were deemed "squatters" when Algonquin Park expanded to include this area in 1914. Their land was taken over and the families were ousted at that time, since they didn't hold formal title.

The McDonald Grave is testament to the trying conditions that early homesteaders faced.

A highly recommended book detailing the early history of the Bonnechere River and Basin Depot area is *Spirits of the Little Bonnechere* by Roderick MacKay.

Basin Road — KM 8.5 to KM 14.4

The present road generally follows the original Basin Road that ran from Eganville to Basin Depot, situated just beyond KM 14. Built in the mid-1800s, Basin Road was an important supply route to the depot that serviced all the logging operations in this area.

In 1967 Martin Garvey, a homesteader's son raised only a few kilometres past the boundary, recollected that in 1909 this road was incredibly busy as a supply route for lumbering operations. As many as 40 teams of horses would pass along this road from 4:00 p.m. until dark. Over the entire day many more teams would have travelled the road.

McDonald Grave — KM 11.2

This grave is marked by a white cross and picket fence. James McDonald cleared the area for farming sometime in the mid- to late 1800s. Alexander McDonald, the infant son of Ronald, a brother of James, was buried here in 1888. The inscription on the cross is still legible. The McDonalds lived on the farm until the provincial government took it over in 1914.

This area was once known as Sligo, after the county in Ireland where Paddy Garvey, another early settler, was born. Sometime after 1855 Garvey set up Sligo House, a stopping place for lumbermen, just south of here along the Bonnechere. After 1870 Garvey concentrated on farming at the next site.

Garvey's Homestead — KM 12.5

Paddy Garvey, who ran Sligo House, farmed here from about 1870 to 1914. As was the case with other "squatters" like the McDonald family, he was uprooted when the Park expanded.

Basin Depot — KM 14.2 to KM 14.4

This open area with two standing buildings has a long and interesting history. The site was important as a central supply and stopover place for lumbermen because it was situated at the junction of two main supply routes. One ran north from Basin Creek to Grand Lake. The other ran parallel to the Bonnechere River to a depot at White Partridge Lake and through to Radiant Lake.

While the exact date of the first building is unknown, in 1843 four shanties were present. By 1890 there were 10 buildings, including a blacksmith shop, a post office and the Basin House, a large building containing a men's bar and living quarters. Between 1949 and 1960 the depot was run by Shoosplin Woods Limited. During this time, 18 buildings stood here and the depot employed 98 men. A ranger cabin, built around the turn of the century, was removed in the 1970s.

This log building is the oldest structure still standing in the Park.

The small log building at KM 14.2 was constructed in 1892 by the McLachlin Lumber Company. Originally built as an office, it served as a hospital during a diphtheria epidemic that same year. In 1909 it was used again as an office by the John D. McRae Lumber Company. After the ownership transferred at least two more times, the structure was employed as a school from 1911 to 1913. The cabin has also served as a harness shop and a summer residence and is the oldest building still standing in Algonquin Park.

Along the east bank of Basin Creek on either side of Basin Road lie two graves enclosed in white picket fences. It is believed that these graves belong to rivermen who drowned during an 1895 spring log drive along the Bonnechere. However, other reports suggest they are graves either of Depot residents or victims of the 1892 diphtheria outbreak.

If you walk to the end of the open area on the south side of the Basin Road directly across from the road to

Basin Lake, you will eventually come to a very pretty spot on the Bonnechere just below where Basin Creek flows into the river.

On the west side of Basin Creek currently stands a large building (apparently scheduled for future demolition and reconstruction in Bonnechere Provincial Park) that was apparently built by the McLachlin Lumber Company. After 1940 it served as a warehouse and storage facility for the Department of Lands and Forests (now the Ministry of Natural Resources). The graves of victims from the 1892 diphtheria outbreak are reportedly located in the poplar grove behind this building.

Foy/McGuey Farm — 1.75 km south from KM 24.4

To reach this old homestead, walk along the logging road that heads south from the Basin Road. The old clearing where the farm buildings once stood is straight ahead along the Bonnechere River when the logging road swings 90 degrees to the right. Although no buildings stand there now, the farm site dates back to the 1870s, when Frank Foy settled the area. In the early 1880s Dennis McGuey took over the farm (as a squatter) and erected a number of buildings, including a stopping place for lumbermen.

CANOEING IN THE BASIN DEPOT

Although not well endowed with canoe routes, the Bonnechere River does offer lovely outings. Along much of its length, the Bonnechere is a meandering, marshy waterway, more creek-like than river-like. Great Blue Herons, American Black Ducks, moose, and otters frequent this river. Be aware in late summer the water levels can be low and sections of the river cannot be paddled. Where navigable, the Bonnechere River, particularly in the northwest sections, offer wonderful day excursions. Canoes can be put in the river at 1.2 km south of KM 30.6, at Little Norway Lake (KM 31.1), at KM 32.2, and where the Bonnechere River crosses the Hydro Line (KM 33.8). One can also launch a canoe outside the Park and paddle into it. One of the best locations for doing so is on the Paugh Lake Road where it crosses the Bonnechere River (2 km past Turner's Camp). Another great location is Couchain Lake (KM 6.5). Also, Basin Lake (1.5 km north of KM 14.2) and Foys Lake (4 km north of KM 23.6) offer good half-day outings.

Basin and Foys lakes are the only sizable bodies of water in the area. Both have access roads that can be rough to travel at times.

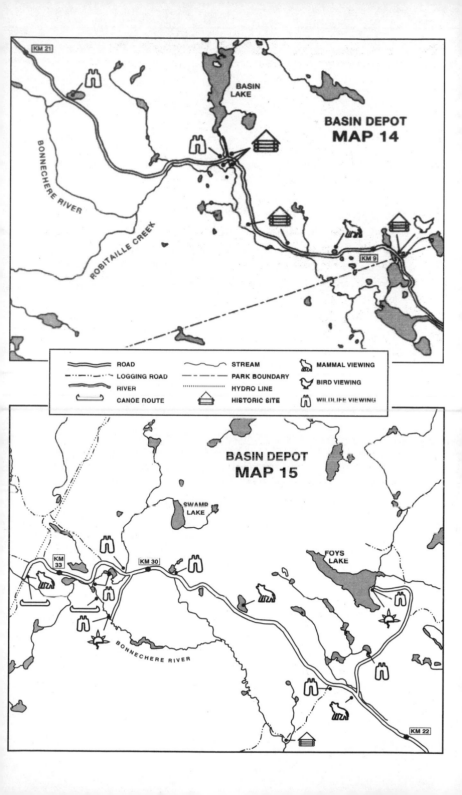

KM 21

BASIN LAKE

BASIN DEPOT
MAP 14

BONNECHERE RIVER

ROBITAILLE CREEK

KM 9

ROAD		STREAM		MAMMAL VIEWING
LOGGING ROAD		PARK BOUNDARY		BIRD VIEWING
RIVER		HYDRO LINE		WILDLIFE VIEWING
CANOE ROUTE		HISTORIC SITE		

BASIN DEPOT
MAP 15

SWAMP LAKE

FOYS LAKE

KM 33
KM 30

BONNECHERE RIVER

KM 22

I N ADDITION to the three main access areas previously profiled (Highway 60 Corridor, East Side and Basin Depot), Algonquin Park can also be entered at a number of other points. Most of these are used primarily for canoe access to the vast Interior and offer few services apart from a permit office and a parking area. However, three of the entrances do have small drive-in campgrounds, and a fourth has campsites within easy walking distance of a parking lot. A relatively new feature available at the three access points detailed below, and at select Interior locations, are ranger cabins that can be rented by the night or by the week. Most of them were built before 1940 by Park Rangers that also used them as overnight accommodation during their travels. A few were used by the men who manned fire towers. At present, 13 rustic cabins are available, with more planned to be upgraded for future rental. Descriptions of the cabins and the rental process are detailed in the free publication, *Old Ranger Cabin Rentals*, available from the Algonquin Provincial Park Information Services (address and phone number are in Appendix 1).

Five Interior access points will be briefly discussed here. Information concerning the remaining access points is detailed in the *Canoe Routes of Algonquin Provincial Park* map brochure available at all retail outlets in the Park, or by mail from The Friends of Algonquin Park (address provided in the appendix IMPORTANT SERVICES). Another useful publication to request is the free *Park Interior Tabloid*.

The majority of the access points are used to start longer canoe trips into the Park Interior. With over 1,500 kilometres of possible routes the Park Interior holds a vast number of both historical and natural history sites. The discussion of all of the known places would require a massive book (or books) and is beyond both the scope and intent of this guide. Only a brief listing of a few of the Interior highlights will be provided, following the brief overview of each Access Point.

KINGSCOTE LAKE

The southern panhandle of Algonquin generally has been one of the most underutilized parts of the park. This was due not to a lack of interesting natural features but to an access road in poor shape and a lack of options apart from canoeing or boating. However, this has changed. The road has been improved and several trails and a number of new campsites have been established. This southern region is well worth a visit (even a day excursion) as its hardwood forests harbour plants and animals that are rare in other parts of Algonquin, and there are some beautiful sites that can be accessed by foot, mountain bike, canoe, or even horse.

There are two ways to enter this part of Algonquin. You can drive on an unpaved road to Kingscote Lake. This 7 km-long road leaves the Elephant Lake Road County Road 10) 13 km north of Harcourt and 22 km west of Maynooth (where County Road 10 is called Peterson Road). You can also access the Park by foot, mountain bike, or horse from the High Falls Parking area, which lies along County Road 10 just 2 km east of the Kingscote Lake Road.

While Kingscote Lake may look like many other Algonquin lakes, it is different in terms of the plant and animal life found near the lake. In early spring the hardwood forests surrounding the lake support a rich assortment of wildflowers that are either rare or not found at all farther north in the Park. From early spring, even before the wild leeks, blue cohosh, and Canada violets have made an appearance, through to the end of summer, the piercing "*keeee-yer, keeee-yer*" calls of Red-shouldered Hawks can usually be heard from the lake. As many as three pairs of this snake-eating hawk, rare

High Falls is reward enough for visiting the Kingscote Lake Region of Algonquin.

through the rest of Algonquin, nest near Kingscote Lake each summer.

The Kingscote Lake Access Point offers two types of campsites. There are more than 20 Interior campsites accessible by canoe on Kingscote and several neighbouring lakes (motorboats with up to 20 horsepower motors are also allowed on Kingscote Lake). There are also a half dozen tenting campsites on the southwest corner of the lake, all situated within 150 metres of a parking lot. There are vault toilets for these walk-in sites but no drinking water or shower facilities.

There are some terrific day canoe trips one can take from Kingscote Lake. From the north-east corner of the lake you can portage into the Minnow lakes (Upper and Lower), or Big Rock Lake. If you are up to the 1300 metre portage that takes you to Big Rock, you will be rewarded. The towering rock cliff for which this lake is named, is spectacular. *The Algonquin Park Canoe Routes* map brochure is essential for any trip as it details not only the portages but also the Interior campsites. Remember, a permit is required to camp and sites must be reserved (1-888-ONT-PARK).

There are two hiking trails accessible from Scorch Lake, which usually takes more than a day's paddle to reach. Leaving the south-east corner of the lake, the kilometre-long Scorch Lake Lookout Trail offers a great view of the lake. Branching off this trail is the two-and-a-half kilometre-long Bruton Farm Hiking Trail. This trail brings you to the site of the Bruton Depot Farm, which was established in 1875. An 80-foot steel fire tower lookout tower, built in the mid-1930s, stood here as well.

A horseback riding trail leads past the Bruton Farm to Lostwater Lake. This trail originates opposite the High Falls parking lot. From the same parking lot two other trails also start. The High Falls Hiking Trail is a very easy trail encompassing less than two kilometres round trip. The first section of the trail is quite level and follows an old road through a pine plantation. The next section that leads to the York River is a foot path. The long rock piles at the base of the rapids are historic glance piers that prevented logs from going ashore during spring log drives. Farther upstream are the spectacular falls, at their magnificent best in spring but worthy of a visit at any time of year..

The Byers Lake Mountain Bike Trail, a 13 km round trip trail, is not particularly difficult as it follows an old logging road. Approximately two thirds of the way to Byers Lake a short, looped hiking trail leads to the east. Bikes are prohibited on this, the Gut Rapids Spur Hiking Trail, which leads to the York River. At Gut Rapids the river flows through a steep, narrow canyon, a must-see for anyone using the bike trail. Algonquin Nordic maintains extensive cross-country ski trails through this part of the Park. The Algonquin Nordic Wilderness Lodge (just outside the Park) offers meals and accommodation in the winter (see **Accommodation** in **Appendix I**).

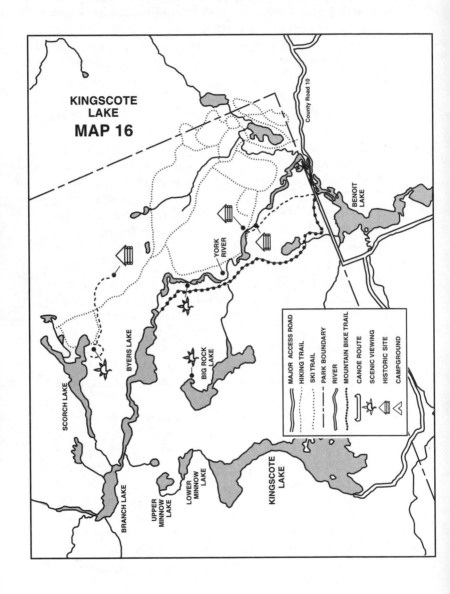

KINGSCOTE LAKE

MAP 16

County Road 10

BENOIT LAKE

YORK RIVER

BYERS LAKE

SCORCH LAKE

BIG ROCK LAKE

BRANCH LAKE

UPPER MINNOW LAKE

LOWER MINNOW LAKE

KINGSCOTE LAKE

MAJOR ACCESS ROAD
HIKING TRAIL
SKI TRAIL
PARK BOUNDARY
RIVER
MOUNTAIN BIKE TRAIL
CANOE ROUTE
SCENIC VIEWING
HISTORIC SITE
CAMPGROUND

All Day Use and Camping permits, as well the *Algonquin South* brochure (with maps for all the trails), the *Canoe Routes of Algonquin Provincial Park* map brochure, and other publications, are available at Pine Grove Point (705-448-2387), situated 0.5 km east of the junction of the Kingscote Lake Access Point Road and County Road 10 (well marked with signs).

BRENT

Situated on beautiful Cedar Lake along the Petawawa River, Brent is the most developed access point in the northern part of Algonquin. There is an outfitting and supply store and a small drive-in campground with only basic facilities (i.e., no flush toilets or showers). There is also a Rustic Ranger Cabin that can be rented. The road into Brent, stretching 40 kilometres from Deux-Rivières on Highway 17, is usually rough and requires slow driving.

At present Brent is a mere shadow of its former self. In earlier years it was a thriving summer recreational and lumbering community. When the railway line (formerly the CNR line that also ran through Achray) was in use, it brought tourists to a popular lodge. Both the lodge and railway line are no longer in existence. Also gone is the sawmill that was the heart of the lumbering industry here.

Apart from access to Cedar Lake and the Petawawa River, the other highlight of the region is the Brent Crater Trail. This is the only interpretive trail in the northern part of the Park. It visits the crater formed when a meteorite crashed here about 450 million years ago.

The trail leads to the bottom of the crater where evidence of the impact, such as shattered rock, can be seen. The trail guide discusses the clues that reveal the origin of the crater. One interesting aspect is that limestone, a rare rock type in Algonquin, is present here. These deposits allow the growth of calcareous plants that are otherwise rare in Algonquin. Some of these, such as bulblet bladder fern, can be found along the trail. A lookout tower on the southeast rim of the crater affords a view of the opposite rim four kilometres away.

161

Permits and a few publications are sold at the Park office located at the junction with Wendigo Lake Road, 24 kilometres before Brent. Motorboats with a maximum 20-horsepower motor are allowed on Cedar Lake.

KIOSK

Kiosk is located on Kioshkokwi Lake, 48 kilometres southwest of Mattawa on Highway 17. Highway 630, the 30.4-kilometre access road from Highway 17, is paved.

At one time Kiosk was a busy town with a sawmill, school and numerous residents. The sawmill, built in 1936, burnt down in 1973 and was rebuilt outside the Park. With the heart of the community gone, the families left one after the other. At the time of writing only one family still resides here, making this once-thriving community virtually a ghost town.

The office is at the lake, just past the rail bed (a remnant of the CNR line that also ran through Brent and Achray). Permits are sold here as well as a few publications. The small campground offers only basic facilities. Just west of the office lies a Rustic Ranger Cabin, which can be rented. Motorboats with a maximum 20-horsepower motor are allowed on Kioshkokwi Lake.

RAIN LAKE

The Rain Lake access point is located 35 kilometres east of Emsdale on Highway 11. The entrance road is unpaved and the small campground has only basic facilities. There is also a Rustic Ranger Cabin for rent near the office where permits and a few publications are sold.

Rain Lake provides access not only to canoe routes but also to the Western Uplands Backpacking Trail. Motorboats with a maximum of 10-horsepower motors are allowed on the lake.

SHALL LAKE

Shall Lake lies 24 kilometres north of Madawaska on Highway 60. The access road is, for the most part, unpaved. There are no drive-in campgrounds or other

A number of the remaining Ranger Cabins, such as this one on Kitty Lake, have been upgraded and can be rented.

facilities here except for the office, which sells permits and a few publications.

The highlight here, though, lies in the easy canoe routes that are accessed from Shall Lake. Some very scenic lakes, such as Shirley and Booth, can be reached with minimal portaging. Many historical sites, including a Ranger Cabin on Kitty Lake (which can be rented), are within easy access. A total of 10 "paddle-in" campsites (areas located a short distance from a drive-in location) are situated on Crotch Lake only a few minutes' paddling time from the canoe launch. Motorboats are not allowed on these waters.

THE PARK INTERIOR

A canoe trip lasting for several days or longer gives one the opportunity to experience Algonquin at its best. To awaken in a dew-covered tent to the sleepy whistles of a White-throated Sparrow allows you to savour the new day as countless thousands of earlier explorers did. To watch a sinking sun set the waters ablaze while the rising wails of loons echo off distant hills is to discover the essence of the Park. Camping in the Park Interior bonds you with the wild in an intimate and unequalled way.

You need not be either an expert canoeist or experienced camper to explore the Park Interior. Common sense and a bit of preparation is all that is required. The outfitters are usually willing to advise you on which equipment will best suit your needs and which routes might be within your time budget. The Park interpretive and Canoe Centre staffs are well versed in Interior travel and are also worth seeking advice from.

Designated campsites are situated along most waterways throughout the Interior. Each has a fire pit as well as a privy of some sort. A maximum of nine people are permitted to camp at a single site. Since all access points limit the number of parties permitted entry each day, it is recommended to reserve access in advance. The Reservation Service number is 1-888-ONT-PARK (1-888-668-7275). The permit-issuing offices for each access point are listed in the *Canoe Routes of Algonquin Provincial Park* map brochure. Remember that in the Interior cans and bottles are banned.

The chapter TIPS FOR THE EXPLORER offers a few basic camping tips. The *Canoe Routes of Algonquin Provincial Park* map brochure is certainly a must for both navigating and camping in the Interior. Also, the map brochure is an important tool for enhancing a canoe trip, since it identifies areas of natural history and historical interest. Another extremely useful Park publication concerning Interior use is the free tabloid *Algonquin Provincial Park: The Park Interior.*

Wildlife-viewing Areas

Wildlife can certainly be encountered on any Interior trip. However, some areas are particularly good for certain species. The following is a brief summary of some of the better locations for seeing animals.

Hailstorm Creek

This extensive boggy creek lies at the northwest corner of Opeongo Lake. To get there can be tricky, for Opeongo is the largest lake in Algonquin and can be extremely rough at times. There is a water taxi service available at the outfitters on Opeongo Lake.

The shallow creek is a favoured moose-feeding area. I have seen as many as 24 moose at one time eating here. Early summer is certainly the best time to see these giants. The creek is also an excellent place to view otters.

Another feature of this boggy area and the next one is the presence of nesting birds that are typically found in farmland outside the Park. Bobolinks and Savannah Sparrows thrive in these large open areas.

Grassy Bay

This boggy creek extending west from the south end of Trout Lake is similar to Hailstorm Creek in habitat but is less productive for moose.

Tim River

This meandering river on the West Side of the Park is excellent for moose in early summer. It also harbours otters as well as many species of northern birds.

Nipissing River

Like the Tim River, this winding waterway is excellent for moose and otters. The stretch between Cedar and Nadine lakes is particularly good.

Catfish Lake

This lake is an important one for moose calving in mid-May and is also significant as a feeding area in early summer. The large boggy marsh between Catfish and Sunfish lakes is excellent for moose and other wildlife in summer.

McCarthy Creek

This creek lies at the southwest corner of Booth Lake. Virtually every species of aquatic plant known in

Algonquin is found here. This rich array attracts moose in early summer.

Hogan Lake

The huge boggy marsh at the southwest end is an excellent summer moose-feeding site.

Other Areas of Natural Significance

A few of the more outstanding areas of natural significance are given here.

Crow River White Pines

This is one of only two areas that still have virgin white pines standing. These magnificent 35-metre-tall trees tower above the nearby hardwoods and can be found approximately two kilometres south of the Crow River just east of Crow Lake.

Dividing Lake White Pines

This is the other area where virgin white pines still grow. Dividing Lake is situated on the southwest border of Algonquin, south of Smoke and Ragged lakes.

Dickson Lake Red Pines

While not as tall as the virgin white pines at Crow and Dividing lakes, the red pines growing on the east side of Dickson Lake are the oldest trees in Algonquin. They are now over 340 years old.

Historical Points of Interest

Due to the vast number of logging camp ruins and other relics from the early days in the Park an entire volume would be needed to cover all of the historical points of interest. Many of these have either become next to impossible to find or can be reached only with extreme effort. The following is simply a listing of some of the more obvious structures that one can easily access during Interior trips.

Barnet Depot and Alligator at Burntroot Lake

Depots were the administrative and supply headquarters for logging companies. Frequently farms were established at these sites to grow potatoes for the men and oats and hay for the horses.

The depot on the southwest shore of Burntroot Lake was built in 1890 by the Barnet Lumber Company and was used until at least 1912. A root cellar and the remains of an alligator are still easily located.

Alligator at Catfish Lake

Parts of an alligator are visible on the island in the northeast corner of Catfish Lake.

Ranger Cabin at Kitty Lake

This cabin, still in excellent condition, was used as a stopover for Park rangers during patrols for poachers and fires.

Ranger Cabin at McKaskill Lake

This cabin is maintained and remains in good shape.

Dennison Farm — East Arm of Opeongo Lake

This farm was cleared in the 1870s by Captain John Dennison, who was killed in 1881 by a black bear caught in a trap and was buried at the farm. The Dennison family moved out of the Park in 1882. The Fraser Lumber Company took over the farm and ran it for a number of years as a depot farm.

Du Fond Farm — Manitou Lake

Ignace and Francis Du Fond cleared this site in 1888. For income they sold produce to logging operations. The farm, which was the last one to be privately owned in the Park, was abandoned in 1916.

McLachlin Depot — Trout Lake

The remains of this depot, built about 1900 by the McLachlin Lumber Company, lie at the northeast corner of Trout Lake.

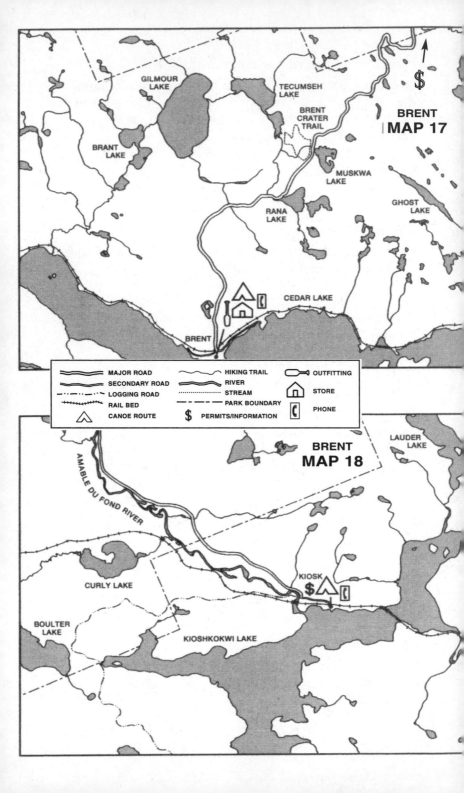

BRENT MAP 17

GILMOUR LAKE

TECUMSEH LAKE

BRENT CRATER TRAIL

BRANT LAKE

MUSKWA LAKE

RANA LAKE

GHOST LAKE

CEDAR LAKE

BRENT

MAJOR ROAD	HIKING TRAIL	OUTFITTING
SECONDARY ROAD	RIVER	STORE
LOGGING ROAD	STREAM	PHONE
RAIL BED	PARK BOUNDARY	
CANOE ROUTE	PERMITS/INFORMATION	

BRENT MAP 18

AMABLE DU FOND RIVER

LAUDER LAKE

CURLY LAKE

KIOSK

BOULTER LAKE

KIOSHKOKWI LAKE

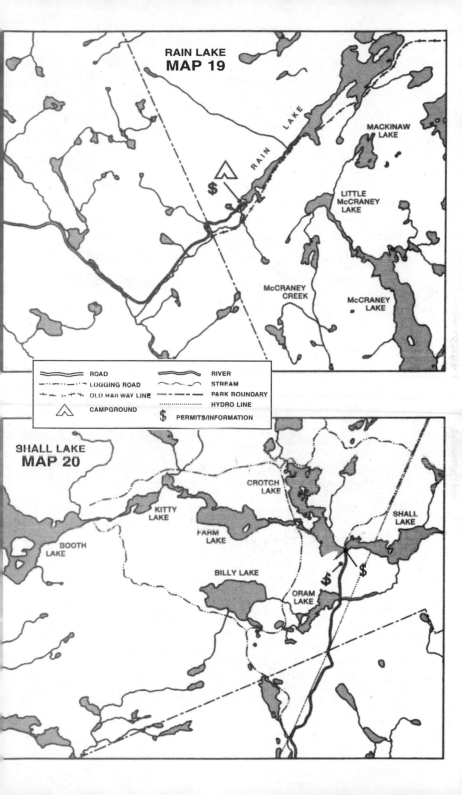

Algonquin Provincial Park is truly a mystical place. Whether it be the wails of a loon rising into the night, the splash of a bull moose munching watershield, the tracks of a wandering wolf crossing soft sand or the scarlet leaves of a red maple blazing against a September sky, the infinite facets of the Park never cease to captivate us. For those who explore its wild reaches Algonquin rewards with an endless array of life-long memories.

But the Park offers more than just natural wonders. Rotting timbers bordering bubbling creeks, mysterious openings in the forest, silent crosses marking unkempt graves — no matter where we roam remnants of another era can be discerned. Like clues in a mystery novel, these markers of a bygone era fuel our imagination and lead us into the past.

If this was your first excursion into Algonquin, I sincerely hope you had the good fortune to experience some of its magic. For anyone who proudly terms himself or herself a "regular," I know you have already fallen under Algonquin's spell. But whether you are making your first or 100th visit, if this book allowed you to leave the Park with an additional fond memory or two, or helped you to avoid a less than desirable experience during your stay, then it has fulfilled its purpose.

May you continue to enjoy this fabulous Park through all the years ahead.

OUTFITTING SERVICES

For outfitters inside the Park the lake on which they are situated is given in brackets. For those outside the Park the nearest town is given. Complete outfitting is provided by all except those marked with an asterisk.

Outfitters within Algonquin

Algonquin Outfitters
(Cedar Lake)
RR #1, Highway 60
Dwight, Ontario
P0A 1H0
705-BRENT-0150
705-635-2243

Alquon Ventures, Inc.
(Canoe Lake)
c/o Huntsville P.O.
Huntsville, Ontario
P0A 1K0
705-633-5622 (summer)
705-789-3645 (winter)

Opeongo Algonquin
(Opeongo Lake)
RR #1, Highway 60
Dwight, Ontario
P0A 1H0
613-637-2075 (summer)
705-635-2243 (winter)

Outfitters outside Algonquin

Algonquin Outfitters
 (Dwight)
RR # 1, Highway 60
Dwight, Ontario
P0A 1H0
705 635-2243

Opeongo Outfitters (Whitney)
Box 123
Whitney, Ontario
K0J 2M0
613-637-5470

Kanukawa Outfitters
(Deep River)
Box 115, RR #31,
Deep River, Ontario
K0J 1P0
613-584-2411

Algonquin Canoe Routes
(Whitney)
Box 187
Whitney, Ontario
K0J 2M0
613-637-2699

Algonquin Portage Store
(Pembroke)
RR #6
Pembroke, Ontario
K8A 6W7
613-735-1795

*Halfway Chute Canoe Rental
(Mattawa)
RR #2, Highway 630
Mattawa, Ontario
P0H 1V0
705-744-2155

Valley Ventures (Deep River)
Box 1115
551 Highway 17 West
Deep River, Ontario
K0J 1P0
613-584-2577
or
RR #1, Braeside, Ontario
K0A 1G0
613-623-7166

Canadian Wilderness Trips
(South River)
187 College Street
Toronto, Ontario
M5T 1P7
416-977-5763

*Poplar Point Camp (Kearney)
Box 99
Kearney, Ontario
K0A 1M0
705-636-5484

Voyageur Outfitting
(South River)
Box 346, Station K
Toronto, Ontario
M4P 2G7
416-488-6175
or
Box 69
South River, Ontario P0A 1X0

Northern Wilderness Outfitters
(South River)
Box 89
South River, Ontario
P0A 1X0
705-386-0466
705-474-3272

*Rickwards Small Motors
(Kearney)
Box 224
Kearney, Ontario
K0A 1M0
705-636-5956

ACCOMMODATION

Only those lodges and motels found either inside or within 20 kilometres of Algonquin will be listed. Of course, numerous other places outside of this arbitrary distance offer accommodation. I would suggest that you contact the Ontario Ministry of Tourism if additional information is required.

Accommodation within Algonquin

Arrowhon Pines Lodge	705-633-5661	or	416-483-4393
Bartlett Lodge	705-633-5543		
Killarney Lodge	705-633-5551	or	416-482-5254
	(summer)		(winter)

Accommodation outside Algonquin

Algonquin Area
Bed and Breakfast
Whitney, Ontario K0J 2M0
613-637-5387

Algonquin East Gate Motel
Box 193
Whitney, Ontario K0J 2M0
613-637-2652

Algonquin Inn and Roadhouse
RR #1
Dwight, Ontario P0A 1H0
705-635-2434
800-387-2244

Algonquin Nordic
1659 Morton Line
RR #1
Cavan, Ontario L0A 1C0
705-745-9497

Algonquin Parkway Inn
Box 237
Whitney, Ontario K0J 2M0
613-637-2760

Algonquin Portage Store
RR #6
Pembroke, Ontario
K8A 6W7
613-735-1795

Bear Trail Inn Resort
Box 158
Whitney, Ontario K0J 2M0
613-637-2662

Blue Spruce Inn
RR #1
Dwight, Ontario P0A 1H0
705-635-2330

Clover Leaf Cottages
RR#1
Dwight, Ontario P0A 1H0
705-635-2049

Curv-Inn
RR #1
Dwight, Ontario P0A 1H0
705-635-1892

Dwight Village Motel/
Coffee Shop
Box 15
Dwight, Ontario P0A 1H0
705-635-2400

Hay Lake Lodge
Box 189
Whitney, Ontario K0J 2M0
613-637-2675

Lakewoods 4 Season Resort
RR #1
Dwight, Ontario P0A 1H0
705-635-2087

Logging Chain Lodge
Box 170
Dwight, Ontario P0A 1H0
705-635-2575

Nor' Loch Lodge
Box 29
Dwight, Ontario P0A 1H0
705-635-2231
800-565-2231

Oxtongue Lake Cottages
RR #1
Dwight, Ontario P0A 1H0
705-635-2951

Parkway Cottage Resort
RR #1
Dwight, Ontario P0A 1H0
705-635-2763

Pine Grove Point**
Harcourt, Ontario K0L 1X0
705-448-2387

Riverside Motel/Restaurant
Dwight, Ontario P0A 1H0
705-635-1677

Riverview Cottages
Box 29
Whitney, Ontario K0J 2M0
613-637-2690

Spring Lake Motel/Restaurant
RR #1
Dwight, Ontario P0A 1H0
705-635-1562

Timber Trail Algonquin
RR#1
Dwight, Ontario P0A 1H0
705-635-1097
800-463-2995

Turner's Camp**
RR #5 Killaloe, Ontario
K0J 2A0
613-757-2672

White Birches Cottage Resort
RR #1
Dwight, Ontario P0A 1H0
705-635-2322

Whitney Cabins
Box 15
Whitney, Ontario K0J 2M0
613-637-2626

**Park Permits sold here

175

Important Addresses and Phone Numbers

For information by mail write to "Information Services" at the address given for the Park Superintendent.

Park Superintendent
Algonquin Provincial Park
Ministry of Natural Resources
Box 219
Whitney, Ontario
K0J 2M0
613-637-2780

The Friends of Algonquin Park
P.O. Box 248
Whitney, Ontario
K0J 2M0
613-637-2828

Camping Reservations
1-888-ONT-PARK
(1-888-668-7275)
Reservation website:
www.OntarioParks.com

Algonquin Park Information
705-633-5572
Web Site:
www.algonquinpark.on.ca
CFOA (Highway 60 radio message): FM 102.7

Algonquin Park Visitor Centre
613-637-2828

Algonquin Gallery
1-800-989-6540 or 705-633-5225 (late June through October)

Bonnechere Provincial Park
1-613-757-2103

Emergency Telephone Numbers

Ontario Provincial Police
1-888-310-1122

Ambulance
Huntsville: 705-789-9694
Barry's Bay: 613-756-3090

Huntsville Hospital
705-789-2311

Barry's Bay Hospital
613-756-3044

Park Staff
(8:00 a.m. to 4:30 p.m.)
705-633-5583
(at other times contact OPP)

Ontario Poison Control
800-267-1373

Fire
705-457-2107

The following is a list of important publications that deal with Algonquin Park. Many other excellent publications are now out of print; only those currently available are given. Because The Friends of Algonquin Park have produced such an excellent series of inexpensive books dealing with Algonquin, a separate section is devoted to these. Other published books appear in the next section.

All of the following publications are available through The Friends of Algonquin Park (see **Appendix 1** for address and phone number).

THE FRIENDS OF ALGONQUIN PARK PUBLICATIONS

I highly recommend these publications as excellent sources of information on specific aspects of Algonquin. Not only are they exceptionally well done but they are also incredibly inexpensive. For example, Birds of Algonquin Provincial Park contains 89 colour photographs and in 1993 sold for a mere $2.95 plus tax.

I also suggest that you purchase the entire set of trail guides. In addition to being essential aids for full enjoyment of the self-guiding trails, they also offer lots of good information about the Park's natural and human history.

Natural History

Birds of Algonquin Provincial Park (Strickland)
Checklist and Seasonal Status of the Birds of Algonquin Provincial Park (Tozer)
Mammals of Algonquin Provincial Park (Strickland)
Wolf Howling in Algonquin Provincial Park (Strickland)
Wildflowers of Algonquin Provincial Park (Strickland and Levay)
Checklist of the Vascular Plants of Algonquin Provincial Park (Brunton and Crins)
Trees of Algonquin Provincial Park (Strickland)
Mushrooms of Algonquin Provincial Park (Thorn)
Checklist of the Conspicuous Fungi of Algonquin Provincial Park (Thorn)
Checklist of the Lichens of Algonquin Provincial Park (Dickson and Crins)
Checklist of the Bryophytes of Algonquin Provincial Park (Crins and Darbyshire)
Reptiles and Amphibians of Algonquin Provincial Park (Strickland)
Checklist of the Butterflies of Algonquin Provincial Park (Reynolds)
Butterflies of Algonquin Provincial Park (Otis)
Insects of Algonquin Provincial Park (Marshall)
The Dragonflies and Damselflies of Algonquin Provincial Park (Holder)

Human History

Algonquin Logging Museum Guidebook (Strickland)
Algonquin Story (Saunders)
Born at Brule Lake (Pigeon)
A Chronology of Algonquin Provincial Park (MacKay)
Early Days in Algonquin Park (Addison)
Glimpses of Algonquin (Garland)
Living at Cache Lake (Pigeon)
More About the Blacksmith's Shop (MacKay)
Pictorial History of Algonquin Provincial Park (Tozer and Strickland)

Miscellaneous

Acid Rain in Algonquin Provincial Park (Strickland)
Algonquin Park Bibliography (Tozer and Checko)
Backpacking Trails of Algonquin Provincial Park (Strickland)
Canoe Routes of Algonquin Provincial Park (Strickland)
Canoeist's Manual (Stringer and Gibson)
Fishing in Algonquin Provincial Park (Strickland)
Joe Lavally and the Paleface (Wicksteed)
Madawaska River and Opeongo River Whitewater Guide (Drought)
Names of Algonquin (Garland)
Petawawa River Whitewater Guide (Drought)
Voices of Algonquin (Tozer and Gibson)
The Best of the Raven (Strickland and Rutter)
The Incomplete Angler (Robins)

OTHER PUBLICATIONS

The following are publications produced by publishers other than The Friends of Algonquin Park.

Natural History

Algonquin Seasons (Runtz)
Moose Country (Runtz)
The Howls of August, Encounters with Algonquin Wolves (Runtz)
Wolf Country (Theberge)

Human History

A Few Rustic Huts (Gage)
Algonquin (MacKay and Reynolds)
Algonquin Adventure (Dickson)
Canoe Lake, Algonquin Park (Shaw)
Lake Opeongo: Untold Stories of Algonquin Park's Largest Lake (Shaw)
Over the Hills to Georgian Bay (MacKay)
Spirits of the Little Bonnechere (MacKay)

Miscellaneous

Algonquin: The Park and Its People (Standfield and Lundell)
Path of the Paddle (Mason)
Song of the Paddle (Mason)
Summer Camp: Great Camps of Algonquin Park (Lundell and Bailey)

Index

accommodation and services, 44-45, 174-176

alligator, 38, 84, 92, 167

archaeological digs, 145

archaeological sites, 94, 95, 134

Achray, 103, 105, 108; campground, 108-109; Merlin, 110

Achray Road: Barred Owl, 121; black bear, 112; red fox, 114

Achray Trail System, 106, 109-110

Airfield, 80, 81; Boreal Chickadee, 69; red fox, 57

Algonquin For Kids, 48

Algonquin Gallery, 38

Algonquin Hotel, 93

Algonquin Logging Museum, 37-38, 46, 49, 83; bookstore, 46; Spirit Walks, 49; trail, 37

Algonquin Portage Store, 104, 107, 130, 169, 170

Algonquin Visitor Centre, 36-37; bookstore, 46; exhibits, 36; interpretive program, 48, 49; restaurant, 45; Wildlife Sightings Board, 50; 76, 176; viewing deck, 9, 76

Arowhon Pines Lodge, 45

aurora borealis, 9

backpacking trails, 42, 106, 162

Barclay Estate, 41, 82, 94

Barnet Depot, 167

Barnet Lumber Company, 167

Barron Canyon Road: access to, 103; blowdown, 126; Interior campsite, 108-109; picnic ground, 107-108; historic sites, 123-130; wildlife viewing, 109-122

Barron Canyon Trail, 104-105

Barron River, 104; canoeing, 106, 131-132; picnic ground, 107

Bartlett Lodge, 45, 76

Basin Depot, 144-155; access, 145; archeological digs, 145; camping, 146; canoeing, 153-154; historic sites, 149-153; maps, 155; permits, 146; wildlife viewing, 146-149; Public Wolf Howls, 148

Basin House, 151

Basin Lake, 146, 154

Bat Lake Trail, 40

beaches: campground 46, 108; picnic ground; 44

bear, black, 10, 11; Basin Depot, 148; East Side, 111-112; Highway 60 Corridor, 57-58; tracks and scat, 17

beaver, 10, 14; Basin Depot, 148; East Side, 114-115; Highway 60 Corridor, 59-61

Beaver Pond Trail, 41

Berm Lake Trail, 105-106, 110

Big Rock Lake, 158

Big Thomson Rapids, 136

bike trails, 41, 157, 159

birds (see also individual species): Basin Depot, 149; etiquette for viewing, 13; East Side, 117-122; Highway 60 Corridor, 62-73; how to call, 14-15; Interpretive walks and talks, 62, publications, 62

biting insects, 26-30

Bittern, American: Costello Creek, 90; Grand Lake, 133; Lake Travers, 136

blowdown, 123, 126, 136

Bobolink: Hailstorm Creek, 147

Bonnechere Provincial Park, 144, 146, 148, 153, 176

Bonnechere River, 144; canoeing, 152-154; drive-in Interior campsites, 146; history of, 150

bookstores, 37, 46

Booth, J.R., 4, 78, 82, 129, 132

Booth's Rock Trail, 41, 76; Barclay Estate, 82

Brent, 161; campground, 161

Brent Crater Trail, 161

Brewer Lake: fall colours, 77; wildlife viewing, 61, 73; wolf howling, 56

Brigham Lake Access, 131

Bruton Farm Hiking Trail, 167

Byers Lake Mountain Bike Trail, 159

Cache Lake, 75, 79

Cache Rapids log chute, 132

183